USS ENTERPRISE (CV-6)
THE MOST DECORATED SHIP
OF WORLD WAR II

Enterprise at the Brooklyn Navy Yard awaiting disposal, June 1958. The newcomer Independence (CV-62) is fitting out across the dock. USN

USS ENTERPRISE (CV–6)
THE MOST DECORATED SHIP
OF WORLD WAR II
A PICTORIAL HISTORY

BY STEVE EWING

Pictorial Histories Publishing Company
Missoula, Montana

LIBRARY OF CONGRESS
CATALOG CARD NUMBER 82-61737

ISBN 0-933126-24-7

First Printing   November 1982
Second Printing   January 1984

Layout by Stan Cohen, Missoula, Montana
Typography by Arrow Graphics, Missoula, Montana
Cover Art Work by Mrs. Diane Ewing Buchannan, Phoenix, Arizona

FRONT COVER:
Her forward elevator blown away and her flight deck broken by a bomb-laden
Kamikaze, the often wounded Enterprise leaves the Pacific war zone for the last time in
May 1945.

BACK COVER:
TOP—Enterprise CV-6 at sea heading for the October 1945 Navy Day ceremonies in
New York City.   NA

MIDDLE & BOTTOM—The after flight decks of the World War II Enterprise CV-6 and
the contemporary Enterprise CVN-65 have been the scenes of destruction and death.
The WWII Enterprise is shown just after the August 1942 Battle of the Eastern
Solomons and the present Enterprise, a Vietnam War veteran, is shown after a series of
accidental explosions on 14 January 1969.   NA and USN

PICTORIAL HISTORIES PUBLISHING COMPANY
713 South Third West
Missoula, Montana 59801

CONTENTS

INTRODUCTION

In the third week of June 1958 this writer, in company with a host of other high school social science students from the southeastern United States, was pushed aboard a tourboat to take a sightseeing trip on the rivers of New York City. Despite the enthusiasm of our chaperones to interest us in historic sights, the week had been a bore because we were too young to appreciate either the efforts of the service club paying our tab or to grasp the meaning of the history we viewed. The primary concern among most of us was whether or not sweethearts back home were "mourning" our absence in the arms of another.

After an hour of looking at tall buildings and dashing inside the tourboat to buy hot dogs and dodge the frequent rainsqualls, the boat's guide announced over the speaker system that something was coming up on our starboard side that all might want to see because very soon we could see it no more: it would be taken away and would be dismantled. The guide, whose voice had been quite matter-of-fact until this time, now spoke in a more interested tone. He informed us that the very large aircraft carrier coming into view was the new 60,000-ton USS *Independence* (CV-62) which was in the process of fitting out. Then he called our attention to the smaller carrier docked beside. "That," he said, "is the famous USS *Enterprise.* You are looking at the most decorated ship of World War Two, the carrier whose planes participated in sinking three of the four Japanese carriers at Midway, that in late 1942 was the only operational carrier in the South Pacific standing between the Marines on Guadalcanal and the Japanese Navy, the first carrier to win the Presidential Unit Citation, and the recipient of a war-time high 20 battle stars. In fact, this ship fought in every major battle in the Pacific except one, was designated as the one ship most symbolic of the U.S. Navy in World War II by the Secretary of the Navy and President, was recognized in a congressional resolution to be worthy of being preserved as a national monument, and. . ." The guide continued to discuss the merits of the Big E, his obvious interest and his wealth of facts drew nearly all on board to the starboard side to witness this ship that would soon cease to exist.

At first the guide's enthusiasm for the *Enterprise* was not matched by his guests. As the tourboat passed directly in front of the *Enterprise* and *Independence,* the *Enterprise* looked like an escort carrier in that the *Independence* was twice as wide, 200 feet longer, and rose higher from the water. One student was heard to say in a mocking tone, "We won World War Two with *that!*"

Indeed, *Enterprise* did not appear to be a terribly profound structure sitting beside the much larger new carrier. On board the *Independence* there were many signs of life as men moved about and large cranes lifted materials onto her deck. Aboard *Enterprise* there were no signs of life. Empty gun tubs, absent radar installations, numerous patches of rust, and raindrops falling from her flight deck added to the desolate and forlorn aura of the condemned warship.

As we moved on the demeanor of the crowd became solemn and all eyes fixed on the rapidly diminishing sight that was *Enterprise.* Just before being completely lost from view, one student's comment captured the thoughts of all: "*Enterprise,* I don't know all that you did, but I thank you."

Several days later on the trip home considerable conversation abounded on the subject "if the *Enterprise* was so famous and congress voted to preserve her as a national monument, then why are they going to scrap her?" Long debate supplied no answer.

Four years later a significant memorial to the ship appeared in the form of a classic book, *The Big E,* written by Commander Edward P. Stafford. The book is classic not only because it tells in depth the great story of the *Enterprise* but also because it was written with an eloquence seldom found in non-fiction literature. Not being fortunate enough to purchase the first edition of *The Big E,* which contained several pictures, or Eugene Burn's *Then There Was One,* a book published during the war recounting *Enterprise's* desperate battles of 1942, the only picture of *Enterprise* in my possession for nearly 20 years was the fading memory of her on that long ago gray day in New York City.

In the past four years this writer has had occasion to talk to a number of the veterans of the *Enterprise* and has been surprised to find that most had no more than one picture of their ship. Some had none. And, many were still wondering why their ship had been lost as a national monument, and wondering what happened to the several parts of the ship that were supposed to have been saved.

Not having been able to erase the poignant experience of June 1958, I have attempted to answer in this book the questions most often forwarded by former crewmembers concerning the last days of the ship. But the primary purpose has been to provide myself, interested readers and, most especially, the surviving members of World War Two's most decorated ship, a pictorial record of the carrier's birth, life, battles and death. Regrettably, *Enterprise* now steams only on the high seas of history, and today she can be visited and viewed only in pictures.

ACKNOWLEDGMENTS

The author would like to express his appreciation to the following for their contribution to this book. Research assistance for the text was provided by Captain John Adams (USN, Ret.), Jim Byrd, John Riley and Richard T. Speer (Naval Historical Center), James W. Cheevers (U.S. Naval Academy Senior Curator), Col. Ernest Biggs (USAF, Ret.), Neal Vermillian (Enterprise Estate), Dr. and Mrs. Frank Badger (University of Charleston Library), Mrs. Elizabeth Scobell (West Virginia State College Library), Mrs. Silva Newman (West Virginia College of Graduate Studies Library), and Miss Ruth Yonelunas.

Photographic research assistance was provided by Agnes F. Hoover and C.R. Haberlein (Naval Historical Center), James Trimble and Paul White (National Archives), Thomas J. Olds (Newport News Shipbuilding), Thomas V. Lake (U.S. Naval Academy Athletic Association), Tom Walkowiak (Floating Drydock), Mrs. Elaine Turner (United Technologies), Sarah Roach (West Virginia Research League), Dr. Neal Blackwood (University of Charleston and veteran of *Antietam*), Jim Roach, Larry Sowinski, Mayor Alfred C. Getler, Dr. and Mrs. Robert King, Dr. Carl C. Hoffmann (son of Henry Hoffmann who supervised the demolition of the *Enterprise*), Bill Ray (*Enterprise* veteran now with the Winston-Salem Journal and Sentinel), and Lawrence E. Seehafer (U.S. Navy).

A special thanks is offered to former *Enterprise* crewmembers who added personal reminiscences. These include retired Admiral John G. Crommelin, retired Admiral Emmett Riera, R.W. Gregory, Bill Ray, Ed Doss, C.J. Flynn, Harrison Welton, W.D. Ferguson, Ken Gaebler, Dave Lister, Frank Albert, James F. Murray, Commander B.H. Beams, Bill Kochever, Jim Barnhill, Guy Trisler, Willie C. Bowdoin, Captain Elias B. Mott, Robert L. Bailey, John LeRoy, Ed White, Art Kropp, Clarence Potter, J.W. Waldron, A.J. Nedzynski, Art Rousseau, John Holland, Bob Piper, Hank Adamson, RADM (Ret.) James D. Ramage, Arlis Hart and Joe Farenelli. Also appreciated were the reminiscences of Dr. Glenn Smith (veteran of *Hornet* CV-12) and Ray Ewing (veteran of *Eastland*).

Dr. Barbara Yeager, Beverly Nall and Karen Hightower took time from their busy academic responsibilities to proof the manuscript and thanks are offered to them. Finally, appreciation is expressed to Dr. Charles Lieble, George Lowry and Stan Cohen for their encouragement and helpful comments.

PHOTO CREDITS

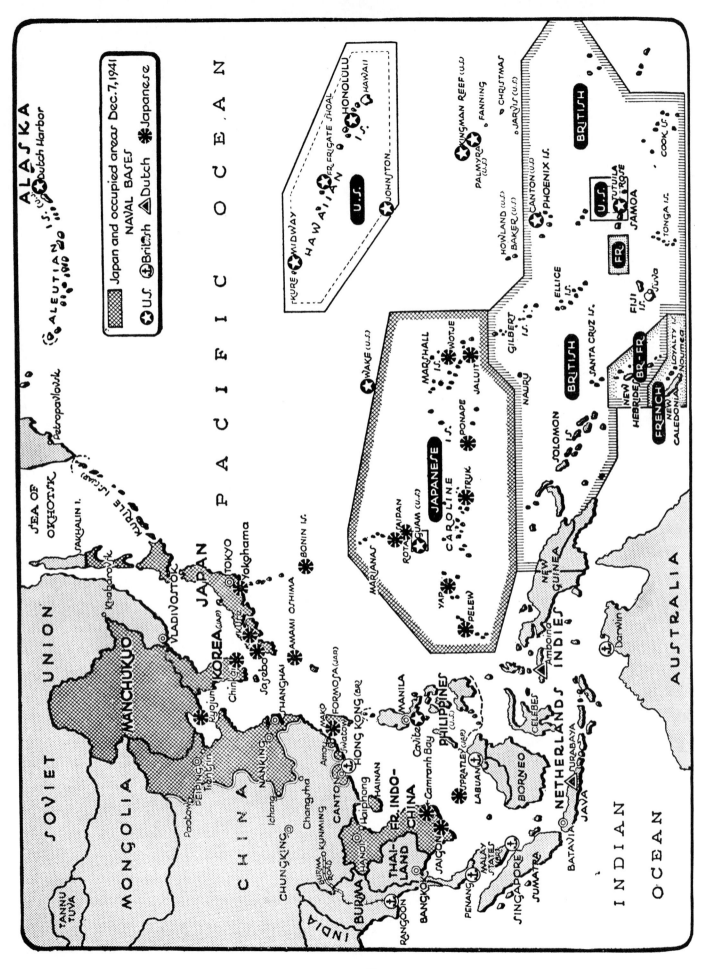

CHAPTER ONE
Before the Storm: 1933-1941

BIRTH OF ENTERPRISE

The year was 1933. For some it was a good year. It was a good year for Franklin D. Roosevelt as he assumed the presidency of the United States; good for Katharine Hepburn and Charles Laughton as they carried home coveted Oscars for their outstanding movie performances; good for Irving Berlin whose most recent hit song was "Easter Parade": and good for John Dillinger who achieved the dubious distinction of being named Public Enemy Number One by the F.B.I.

For many Americans—especially the over 12 million unemployed—1933 was not a good year. The United States and the industrial world were in the fourth year of the great depression and extraordinary events in the nation's capital pointed to the serious tone of the times. On 6 March all banks in the country were closed and on 9 March the special 100 days session of congress began. When the special session ended on 16 June the government had passed the New Deal legislation, which has since deeply affected the economic and social life of all Americans. And buried deep in part of this historic legislation was an allocation for approximately $19 million of a total naval construction allocation of $238 million to build what would soon become one of the most successful warships of all time.

Development of aircraft carriers in the United States, Great Britain and Japan had already passed the incipient stage by 1933. America's first carrier, *Langley*, a converted collier commissioned in March 1922, was long obsolete by 1933. The U.S. Navy did have in service two big (33,000 tons), fast, relatively new and efficient carriers in *Lexington* (CV-2, commissioned December 1927) and *Saratoga* (CV-3, commissioned November 1927). Both had been converted from their original battlecruiser design due to the restrictions imposed by the 1922 Washington Naval Treaty. And in February 1933 America's first carrier designed and built as a carrier from the keel up, *Ranger* (CV-4, 14,400 tons) was launched. Still, the provisions of the Washington Naval Treaty alloted another 55,000 tons of the original 135,000 tons to the United States for aircraft carriers, and the Navy had been planning since 1931 to build two new 19,800-ton carriers that would incorporate all the technology and lessons learned from experience with the first four.

On 21 May 1934 the keel of the first of the two newly authorized carriers, *Yorktown* (CV-5), was laid down at Newport News Shipbuilding and Dry Dock Company. With less fanfare the keel of the second, *Enterprise* (CV-6), was laid down on 16 July 1934. To Newport News from all points of the compass came steel, copper, Douglas fir and the other resources that when assembled would displace nearly 20,000 tons of water and would form a vessel 809 feet long and 109 feet wide across its wooden flight deck. In the following four years hundreds of men paid by Public Works Administration funds would devote their attention to the construction of the sister ships unaware that their individual and collective skills would create in *Yorktown* a heroic ship fate would prematurely commit to Valhalla and would create in *Enterprise* the United States Navy's most decorated ship in World War Two.

Yorktown was launched on 4 April 1936 and there to do the honors was no one less than the wife of the President, Mrs. Franklin D. Roosevelt. Six months later on 3 October 1936 *Enterprise* slid down the ways. Although not quite the media attraction of her sister ship, a good size crowd and numerous dignitaries watched Mrs. Claude A. Swanson, wife of the Secretary of the Navy, christen the ship with prophetic words borrowed from Shakespeares' *Othello*: "May she also say with just pride: I have done the State some service."

Service to the State for *Enterprise* began soon after her commissioning date of 12 May 1938 when she steamed to Brazil on her shakedown cruise under the command of her first mentor, Captain Newton H. White, Jr. Upon return the ship was ordered to participate in winter maneuvers in the Caribbean and soon thereafter (21 December 1938) received aboard the man generally recognized as most responsible for the ship's high level of pre-war training and efficiency, Captain C.A. Pownall.

By December 1938 it was obvious to Capt. Pownall and most other ranking officers of the Navy that *Enterprise* and other ships of the fleet built by New Deal financed programs might soon have a more immediate and special meaning than the new post offices, Civilian Conservation Corps, Tennessee Valley Authority, federal buildings and bridges. Clouds of war which were thin, white and high at the time of *Enterprise's* authorization in 1933 were in late 1938 broad, gray and low. Although popular magazines of the time focused on better economic times and informed readers that a new Plymouth could be had for only $25 a month and that $800 would purchase an eight-cylinder Oldsmobile, they also devoted spacious sections to the ominous signs of coming conflict. In the few short years of life for *Enterprise,* Adolph Hitler's Germany had reinstated conscription, had occupied the Saar and Rhineland and had moved to annex Austria. Spain had become embroiled in a bloody civil war, and in the Far East the conflict between Japan and China was increasing in ferocity and scope. And soon after *Enterprise's* launching date in 1936, Japan terminated the naval treaties of 1922 and 1930 thereby opening the doors to an arms race which the United States Navy joined in earnest in 1938.

While crew members aboard the U.S. Navy's newest carrier trained vigorously to operate their ship effectively, the three-year period from *Enterprise's* commissioning to war was also the time in which aircrew personnel were honing their skills for the ultimate test. Aerial combat tactics were refined and innovations implemented, but the major advancement between 1938 and 1941 was in rapid improvement of carrier aircraft. *Enterprise* had been designed and built at a time when carrier aircraft were light, relatively slow biplane types, many with fixed (non-retractable) landing gear. By 1938 the majority of planes were still biplanes, the Northrop BT-1s (bomber) and Douglas Devastator TBDs (torpedo-bomber) being the only monoplanes to operate from the decks of carriers at the time of *Enterprise's* commissioning. By 1941, however, all biplanes had flown from Enterprise's deck for the last time. On board in December 1941 were new F4F Grumman Wildcat fighters, Douglas Dauntless SBD dive bombers (both would fight through the entire war), and the TBD torpedo planes which, regrettably, would be devastated in their last battle —Midway—only six months into the war.

Enterprise moved into the Pacific, the ocean of peace, to base at San Diego in April 1939; but just after Germany's invasion of Poland and the outbreak of general war in Europe (September 1939) the ship headed west and steamed to her new base of operations. . .Pearl Harbor. Although training was the main order of business in the three pre-war years for *Enterprise,* considerable time was devoted to transporting aircraft, Army planes as well as Navy, from the mainland of the United States to Pearl Harbor and other Pacific bases. The final days of peace for the carrier were spent on one such mission and disconcerting as these transport duties were, the final such mission was to be a very considerable blessing in disguise. But before that mission men aboard *Enterprise* would train with purpose and emotion, participating in the final fleet problems and war games with distinction.

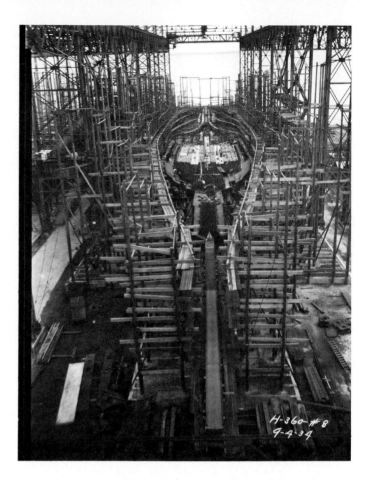

Enterprise *building at Newport News Shipbuilding and Dry Dock Company, Virginia, 1934-1936.*
NNSDDC

Enterprise *building at Newport News Shipbuilding and Dry Dock Company, Virginia, October 1, 1936.*
NNSDDC

THE JAPANESE NAVY

On the eastern side of the Pacific Ocean other war games and fleet problems were in progress in the late thirties and into 1941. Other men aboard other carriers converted from battlecruisers (*Akagi* and *Kaga*) and aboard new carriers (*Soryu, Hiryu, Shokaku* and *Zuikaku*) carrying birth dates approximating those of *Yorktown* and *Enterprise* were training with purpose and emotion equal to if not in excess of that of the U.S. Navy. The rising sun of Japan was indeed on the ascent and it shone brightly on the heretofore undefeated fleet of the "Land of the Gods."

At the time of the Japanese decision to modernize in the latter years of the 19th century the unquestioned major naval power in the world was Great Britain. In fact, Great Britain was the world leader in many areas of endeavor including colonization, industrial development (with Germany and the United States) and overall international economic and political import. It was the Japanese desire to learn from the best and so it was that the Japanese Navy developed along British lines. Many of the early Japanese naval vessels were designed and built by the British, the Japanese Naval Academy was fashioned after that of Britain, and discipline and decorum too followed the pattern of the British. Indeed, the British example was observed to the extent that the unwritten rule of the captain going down with his ship was practiced so often that the Japanese unnecessarily lost many top commanders.

Japanese naval tradition got off to a rousing start in the 1904-1905 war with Russia. Arriving unannounced and without a declaration of war, the

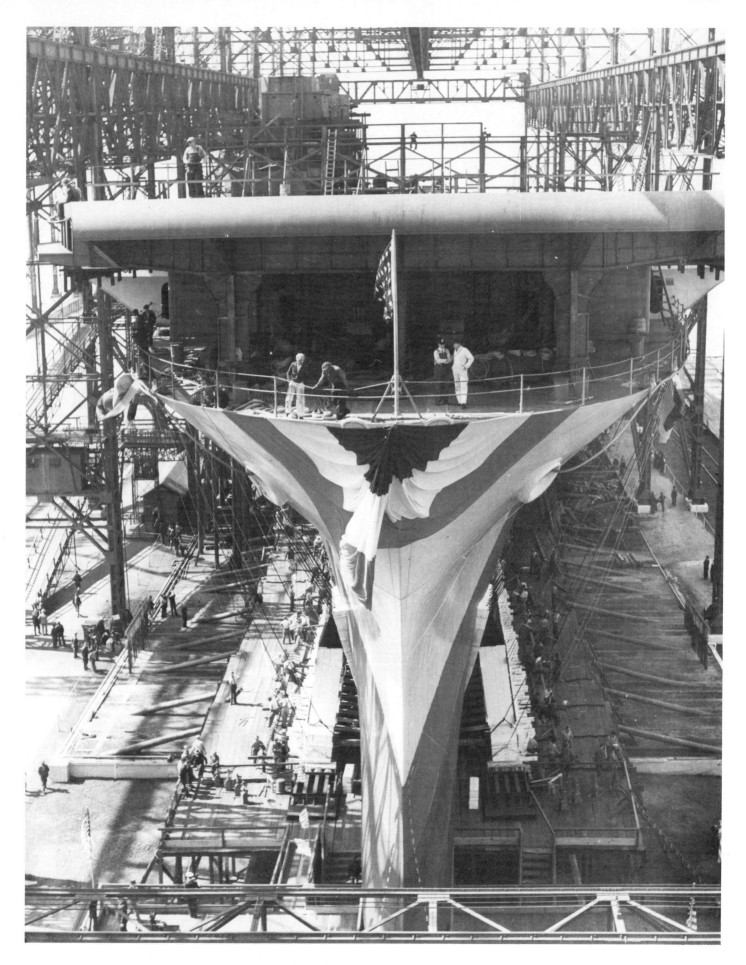

Final preparations for launch, October 1936. NA

Enterprise *clear of the ways.*   NNSDDC

Enterprise *is christened by Mrs. Claude A. Swanson, wife of the Secretary of the Navy, 3 October 1936.*
USN and NNSDDC

-5-

Sister ships Enterprise *and* Yorktown *at Newport News while fitting out, 1938.*   NA

Japanese battle fleet steamed into Port Arthur during the night of 8 February 1904 and attacked capital ships of the Czar's navy. Then on 27 May 1905 the Japanese Fleet under the direction of Admiral Togo (with young Ensign Isoroku Yamamoto on board the flagship) executed the classic crossing of the T at the battle of Tsushima and all but annihilated the remainder of the Russian Fleet which had sailed from the Baltic Sea halfway around the world in an attempt to avenge the Port Arthur disaster. The battle of Tsushima transferred the long-honored spirit of the samurai from strictly a land connotation to the sea. Indeed, this "spirit of Tsushima" would express itself time and again in the numerous battles of the early 1940's.

Immediately prior to the outbreak of war the Japanese Fleet compared favorably to that of the United States. In some areas, i.e., aircraft carriers and modern battleships, the Japanese had a definite quantitative edge. Wartime shipbuilding programs in the United States would far exceed the Japanese capacity, but in 1941 the soon-to-be combatants were a fairly even match in total naval strength.

Although relatively even in number of ships, the period just before the beginning of hostilities found the Japanese well ahead of American thinking concerning the utilization of carrier-borne air power. The carrier was an offensive weapon in the minds of many Japanese sea commanders that could, should and would be used as a separate striking force. To the contrary, many American commanders in 1941 believed the primary role of the carrier was to be supportive of battle fleet operations. Later in the war this belief had expression, and properly so. But during the incipient stage of the war it was the Japanese who would provide the lessons on the potential of the carrier as an offensive weapon.

Enterprise *one month before her commissioning date, April 1938.* USN

Enterprise *in 1939. Note original bridge configuration.* USN

Secretary of the Navy Frank Knox on flight deck of Enterprise *inspecting Northrop BT-1 bomber circa 1940.*   USN

THE JAPANESE CARRIERS AND ENTERPRISE

World War Two in the Pacific was a carrier war. Success or failure of the respective antagonists aircraft carriers determined overall strategy, especially during the first year of the war, and eventually sealed the fate of Japan's war fortunes.

At the end of the war historians would be able to count 20 carriers plus at least four escort carriers having served in the Japanese Navy. However, the burden of fighting fell on only 14 of these ships. The carriers that would engage American forces to trade bombs, torpedoes and bullets included the six pre-war large fleet carriers *Akagi, Kaga, Hiryu, Soryu, Shokaku* and *Zuikaku* and the light carriers *Ryujo, Zuiho, Shoho, Ryuho, Junyo, Hiyo, Chitose* and *Chiyoda.* Only two large fleet carriers, *Taiho* and *Shinano*, were commissioned by the Japanese during the war. *Taiho* died early in her first battle (June 1944 by USN sub *Albacore*), and *Shinano* too was sunk by an American submarine (*Archerfish*) before she was ready to enter combat (November 1944). The light carriers *Unryu, Amagi* and *Katsuragi* were available in 1944 but lacking aircrews they never

struck any blows at United States forces, *Unryu* being sunk by USN submarine *Redfish* in December 1944 while *Amagi* and *Katsuragi* were bombed in port in the waning days of the war. Japan's first carrier, *Hosho*, was too small, slow and ill-armed for combat and sailed only once toward the scene of battle (Midway) but encountered no action. Finally, Japan would lose four escort carriers (*Chuyo, Taiyo, Unyo* and *Shinyo*) to American submarines in 1943 and 1944. None of the four ever engaged an American carrier.

Enterprise engaged 12 of the 14 Japanese carriers active in combat. The Big E would sink *Akagi* and *Kaga* in their only meeting at Midway, would share credit with planes from sister ship *Yorktown* in the sinking of *Hiryu*, would fight *Zuikaku* and *Zuiho* four times, *Shokaku* three, *Junyo, Hiyo, Chitose* and *Chiyoda* twice, *Ryuho* and *Soryu* once. Although it is not possible to know exactly which ship to credit for the wounds suffered in battle by *Enterprise*, it is known that her seven major and nine minor wounds occurred while fighting enemy carriers *Zuiho, Zuikaku, Shokaku* and *Junyo*, occurred while battling Japanese land-based planes and occurred finally as a result of being hit by American anti-aircraft shells.

Japanese aircraft carrier Akagi *in April 1939.* Akagi *was the enemy flagship at Pearl Harbor and Midway.*

THE FUTURE FOE

During the 7 December 1941 attack by the Japanese on Pearl Harbor, one American serviceman was quoted as saying "I didn't even know they were sore at us!" He was not alone. Although most Americans realized there were problems between the two nations, few fully appreciated the severity of the differences and even fewer recognized the probability that the United States would become involved not only in the European war but also, the "China Incident." Indeed, the problems did not develop overnight. Rather, they developed over a period of approximately 50 years and grew in a manner that would require settlement in the final court of appeal...war.

The initial relations between the United States and Japan were not bad even if they were a bit unusual. Needing coaling stations and wishing to investigate reports of mistreated shipwrecked sailors in the Japanese islands, the United States entrusted Commodore Matthew Perry with a mission to Japan to open negotiations on these and other matters. Arriving in 1854 Perry began the process that led to relations between the two countries and helped initiate the process of bringing the Japanese to the realization that their self-imposed isolation dating from 1620 was no longer a practical foreign policy. Between 1854 and 1868 Japanese leaders observed the dynamic technological changes that had occurred during their isolation and recognized they would be relatively powerless to fend off a significant imperialistic thrust at their sovereignty. The Japanese were also quick to recognize that the nations of the world in the latter part of the 19th century were falling into two catagories: those who possessed colonies and those who were colonized. By 1868 the internal debate on revoking the policy of isolation was over (thanks in part to the several occasions when western nation navies bombarded Japanese coastal villages whose inhabitants continued to mistreat shipwrecked sailors—a lesson not lost on the perceptive Japanese who would use similar tactics in the not too distant future.).

After 1868 the Japanese turned quickly to the task of modernization. Many of the best intellects available were sent to the industrialized nations of Europe and America to learn the ways of the modern world. Chief among their assignments was to observe military structure and to learn how to build warships, sail them, and use them in combat. The traditional industriousness of the Japanese people was evident as men of the samurai spirit accomplished their orientation and learning tasks with enthusiasm and distinction. Within 27 years of the 1868 Mei ji Restoration, Japan engaged in war the world's most populous country, China, and won. Ten years later (1904-1905) the Japanese fought the world's largest country in land area, Russia, and

Akagi *and battleship* Kongo *circa 1927 before the carrier's modernization.*   USN

won. The victory over Russia was significant; it was the first time in modern history that an oriental people had defeated a European country. And the victory over Russia gained Japan the status of an international power, albeit not a power of the first rank.

Relations between the United States and Japan, which had been favorable in the latter portion of the 19th century, began to turn sour when at the peace conference between Japan and Russia, United States President Theodore Roosevelt served as mediator. The strength of Roosevelt's position enabled him to impose ideas which led to the signing of a peace treaty and garnered for him the Nobel Peace Prize. However, his actions were not well received by the Japanese who left the negotiations feeling Roosevelt had taken from them gains won on the battlefield and sea. Also, it was about this time that the Japanese began to perceive a feeling of racial discrimination in dealings with representatives of the American government. Only a few years later American congressional legislation restricting immigration quotas of orientals converted perceptions of discrimination to documented belief of same. And the Washington Naval Treaty of 1922 assigned inferior status to the Japanese with a 5-5-3 capital ship-ton ratio for the United States, Britain and Japan, respectively.

The great war in Europe fought between 1914 and 1918 found the Japanese on the same side with France, Great Britain, the United States and other allies but the Japanese role in the conflict was peripheral. The Japanese contribution of note to the war effort centered on their taking possession of several remote Pacific island groups claimed by Germany. These islands—the Marshalls, Carolines and Marianas were not the central concern of the representatives of the victorious allies at the Versailles Treaty proceedings and Japan's request that these islands be mandated to them for their support of the allied cause met with acceptance after some heated debate.

Many students of the 1920-1940 era cite the onset of the world depression as the catalyst for Japanese expansionist moves beginning in 1931 with the invasion of Manchuria in northeastern China. Unquestionably, the depression was a major factor, perhaps the most significant factor, in the actions of the Japanese. However, a host of cultural attributes ranging from the influence of the Shinto religion to the traditional militaristic inclination of important sectors within the national leadership contributed to the events which would culminate in the Pacific war.

Although the League of Nations condemned

Manchurian invasion it did not have the power to take any other action. Japan gave notice of withdrawal from the League in 1933 and by 1937 Japan and China were engaged in full-scale war. The United States and the countries of Europe were occupied by problems of the depression and the more pressing potential of conflict in Europe as resurgent Germany asserted her will to undo the provisions of the Treaty of Versailles. The oriental mind has never been impressed with threats; action, yes; words, no. Therefore, the many notes of protest were read, acknowledged and then left to diplomats for debate. Words began to draw notice, however, in 1936 when the tone of the notes from the United States turned firm. Japanese response, in part, was to withdraw from all naval treaties completely and to begin a major shipbuilding program, increase the size of the armed forces and step up propaganda messages to her people. The basic propaganda theme was the inevitability of war with western countries determined to keep Japan from her proper place on the world stage, to keep her from her rightful position as economic and political leader in the orient, and to prevent her from obtaining needed living space and resources for a rapidly expanding population.

By 1938 words from the United States became action. Congressional appropriations signaled the major thrust of American military preparedness. War games were not fought against an ambiguous aggressor; they were designed with Japan in mind.

By 1940 diplomacy had become diplomatic war and was underway in full force. In May 1940 major portions of the U.S. Pacific Fleet were ordered to operate indefinitely in the Hawaiian area, an action considered belligerent by the Japanese. In July 1940 the Export Control Act was invoked cutting off the export of petroleum products, scrap metal and other essentials to Japan. In May 1941 an unlimited national emergency was declared and in July 1941 came the strongest diplomatic move of all; Japanese assets were frozen. This last diplomatic act was in essence an ultimatum. The Japanese were cut off from vital resources and the choice left to them was (1) acquiesce to American demands and withdraw from China or (2) seize southeast Asia and thereby gain access to needed resources. Although there were Japanese leaders who wanted to avoid war (including the man who would plan the attack on Pearl Harbor, Admiral Isoruko Yamamoto) the militarists—primarily the Army leadership—had the upper hand as they had already demonstrated their willingness to assassinate top-ranking figures opposed to a peaceful solution. And one cannot overlook the aversion of any Japanese to the possibility of "losing face" by backing down from American demands.

The major problem with the second alternative—seizing southeast Asia—was the presence of the American-controlled Philippine Islands directly between Japan and the coveted countries. To counter the expected American resistance to their moves Admiral Yamamoto proposed a departure from the long-held plan of how to fight a war with the United States, i.e., let the U.S. Navy sail across the Pacific to battle the Japanese Fleet in home waters with the Japanese possessing the advantages of interior lines. Yamamoto's new plan, received without enthusiasm by most of his staff, focused on a pre-emptory attack against the American Fleet at Pearl Harbor in the hope of buying sufficient time to (1) take the resource-rich areas of southeast Asia, (2) erase the American presence in the Philippines and establish Japanese bases in their place, and (3) establish an outer defense by taking additional islands in the north, central and south Pacific. And it was Yamamoto's hope to damage the American Fleet to such a degree that the United States in time would agree to a negotiated peace instead of paying the price of rebuilding a fleet and sacrificing the many lives necessary to fight across the entire Pacific.

Practically all historians who have written on the subject agree in retrospect that Yamamoto's strategic plans would have had a greater chance for success had he not decided on the Pearl Harbor attack. The attack, launched before a declaration of war, inflamed the American soul and united the country toward one purpose...revenge and victory.

That war would come and that it would involve Pearl Harbor were subjects discussed in writing on more occasions than one. In 1925 a book entitled *The Great Pacific War* by Hector C. Bywater detailed the upcoming war, complete with a description of a surprise attack on Pearl Harbor. General Billy Mitchell in 1925 declared Pearl Harbor vulnerable to attack, and war games by the U.S. Navy in the 1930s proved his point. Further, for nearly ten years prior to the attack, final examinations at the Japanese Naval Academy included a question asking how the future officers would plan an attack on Pearl Harbor. And, aboard the United States newest aircraft carrier in the Pacific, USS *Enterprise,* was posted the first war order for the U.S. Navy in World War Two 10 days before the attack.

Enterprise *in Hawaii, 1940.*   USN

Admiral Halsey escorts Lord Louis Mountbatten to a seat on the hangar deck of Enterprise *in 1941. Mount-batten spoke on the recent sinking of his destroyer and then a movie was shown. The movie ended abruptly when a secret homemade moonshine still blew up in the projection booth.*   Courtesy of John LeRoy

CHAPTER TWO
Pearl Harbor

The story of America's unpreparedness for war both at Pearl Harbor and throughout the country has been told many times and does not need to be retold in depth here. However, the reader will no doubt find it interesting to look through magazines published in the days prior to the attack to get a feel for the attitude of the time. The broad essence of the articles pertaining to problems in Asia centered on the theme of Japan as an unworthy opponent in war. Stories of this type were documented with pictures showing Japanese tankettes and other seemingly inferior weapons. The articles, however, did not carry many pictures or stories of the efficient Zero fighter plane, the two new over 65,000-ton superbattleships, Japan's two latest excellent aircraft carriers *Shokaku* and *Zuikaku,* and little was said concerning the fanatical fighting spirit of the Japanese soldier and sailor. Even radio broadcasts the day of the attack continued the theme that "everything would be alright very soon." Long-held ideas die hard.

As *Enterprise* and the Japanese raiding force converged on Pearl Harbor from the west and northwest respectively, the 8 December 1941 issue of *Life* magazine was being readied for distribution on American newstands the coming Monday morning. On the cover of this issue was a picture of General Douglas MacArthur and it contained a nine-page spread on life aboard an aircraft carrier in the Pacific. The pictures displayed and the words described *Enterprise.* It's ironic that this story about *Enterprise* appeared in a major magazine being printed on the day of the Pearl Harbor attack. For the Japanese attack sought to destroy the ship that would play a significant role in the following years of war.

In the two-plus years *Enterprise* had been stationed at Pearl Harbor much of her time had been consumed in transporting supplies and the materiel of war to outlying bases throughout the Pacific. On the 28th of November 1941 she departed Pearl on what would be her last such mission. On this voyage she had been ordered to ferry a squadron of U.S. Marine pilots and their planes to bolster the defense of Wake Island. On the evening of the 28th the following written order was placed into the hands of the carrier's pilots:

BATTLE ORDER NUMBER ONE

1. The *Enterprise* is now operating under war conditions.
2. At any time, day or night, we must be ready for instant action.
3. Hostile submarines may be encountered.
4. The importance of every officer and man being specially alert and vigilant while on watch at his battle station must be fully realized by all hands.
5. The failure of one man to carry out his assigned task promptly, particularly the lookouts, those manning the batteries, and all those on watch on deck might result in great loss of life and even the loss of the ship.
6. The Captain is confident all hands will prove equal to any emergency that may develop.
7. It is part of the tradition of our Navy that, when put to the test, all hands keep cool, keep their heads, and FIGHT.
8. Steady nerves and stout hearts are needed now.

The order was signed by Captain George D. Murray and approved by Admiral William (Bill) F. Halsey.

Ten days before the attack on Pearl Harbor Admiral Halsey and *Enterprise* were at war. The timing was good because the Japanese raiders had departed northern Japan two days earlier (26 November) bound for Hawaii and World War Two.

The Japanese had done their homework in preparing for the surprise attack. Spies fed information on the status of the American Fleet in Hawaii back to Japan until hours prior to the shooting. Last minute technical innovations provided a shallow-water torpedo that would be immensely successful against American battleships, and two Japanese naval officers traveling incognito had just sailed the planned northerly route and had not encountered ships of any nation. The possibility of surprise appeared favorable. Hopes rose that the Emperor's navy would be able to sink battleships within the harbor, sink and damage several cruisers, cripple Army and Navy air power in the area and, best of all, catch either *Enterprise* or *Lexington*—America's only two carriers based at Pearl—in port.

On 2 December the 12 Marine planes flew from

U. S. FLEET
COMMANDER AIRCRAFT, BATTLE FORCE

HEADING: OOTH V 2GMF Z FSL 071830 CSQ TART O BT

URGENT   _URGENT_   _URGENT_

3146 M.I.N.Y. 4-14-37—100M. sets of 9

AIR RAID ON PEARL HARBOR X THIS IS NOT DRILL.

FONED TO SOO 1842/WF   TOR 1840 WB 4295

NITE	Unless Checked Otherwise	ROUTINE	PRIORITY	ACK	CONFIRM	RADIO	VISUAL	MAIL	
FROM:	CINCPAC				DATE 7 DEC 1941	SUPR. KY	C.W.O.	NR.	
ACTION:	ALL SHIPS PRESENT HAWAIIAN AREA.							RELEASE	CORREES FILE
INFO:									

ADMIRAL

"This copy of the historic message reporting the attack on Pearl Harbor was recorded aboard the Enterprise _by W.D. Ferguson. Ferguson recalls that he initially believed the message to be a drill despite the disclaimer. He also recalls that Admiral Halsey immediately accepted the message as genuine."_ W.D. Ferguson

the deck of _Enterprise_ toward Wake Island, and the big carrier swung around and headed back to Hawaii. Several hundred miles to the north the Japanese Fleet too was headed for Hawaii with an expected arrival time for her planes over the American anchorage at 7:55 Sunday 7 December. _Enterprise_ was due in the harbor on Saturday afternoon 6 December. Both were on schedule.

It has been said many times in many different ways that the best-made plans of men are subject to the winds of fortune. In those last days of peace in 1941 a large weather system over the north Pacific would literally become the winds of fortune for both the approaching Japanese Fleet and the homeward-bound _Enterprise_. The overcast weather covered the Japanese raiders while clear skies over east Asia and southeast Asia allowed observers to track naval units moving from Japan toward the Philippines and the Dutch East Indies (Indonesia). This, of course, centered attention on the Far East and therefore added to the element of surprise for the Hawaii attack.

This same weather system, however, stirred the waters west of Hawaii and thereby affected the course of _Enterprise_ and her 11 attendant cruisers

and destroyers. The rain and rough seas did not impede the progress of _Enterprise_ or the cruisers _Northampton, Salt Lake City_ and _Chester,_ but it made life miserable aboard the eight destroyers. Admiral Halsey, who would fight the first six months of the war with his flag flying from the distinctive tripod mast of _Enterprise,_ had served on destroyers and knew their plight. Being sensitive to the welfare of his men and the possibility of damage to the destroyers, he ordered reduced speed. So it was that inclement weather, rough seas and Halsey's empathetic order spared the lives and ships of the _Enterprise_ task force. And just as many blessings arrive in disguise and are not appreciated at the moment of occurrence, it was the same aboard _Enterprise_ and the three cruisers. The reduced speed meant no Saturday night in port, no Saturday night on the town, and no quiet Sunday of leisure.

WAR

The first day of war for _Enterprise_ would prove to be long and eventful. It would also prove to be a day in which "Murphy's Law" (if something can go

Aerial view of Ford Island and the Battle Fleet in Pearl Harbor 8 April 1938.

Enterprise *and cruiser* Salt Lake City (CA-25) *at Pearl Harbor 25 October 1939.*

wrong, it will) was in full force. December 7, 1941 was in no way a good day for *Enterprise* except for the fact that she did not arrive in the harbor as originally scheduled.

The day began normally as a squadron of SBD's left the deck at sunrise to scout ahead and then land on Ford Island. The scouts would arrive approximately six hours before the ship and by noon the entire *Enterprise* task force would be home. However, shortly after 8 o'clock the first reports of the battle in progress came to *Enterprise* via one of her own scout planes. The report was not formal and it was not directed back to the carrier: it was instead a plea. "Please don't shoot! This is an American plane." Minutes later from the base came official word: "Air raid Pearl Harbor—This is no drill."

The only U.S. Navy planes in action over Pearl Harbor during the battle were the scout planes from *Enterprise*. Regrettably, they too were on the receiving end of the action instead of the giving side. Unaware of what they were flying into they were caught by surprise. And their planes were bombers. Perhaps a different historical account would have been recorded that day had the scout planes been fighters. The result of the battle would not have changed but the Japanese most likely would have suffered at least the losses sustained by the *Enterprise* squadron. As it was only two Japanese planes are believed to have been downed by *Enterprise* planes. The attempted landings by *Enterprise* planes on Ford Island during the morning attack and later when returning in darkness after searching for the enemy resulted in the loss of nine planes, six pilots and several aircrew personnel. Only two of the planes were downed by the Japanese; the others were downed by American gunfire.

Aboard the carrier, still 150 to 200 miles west of Hawaii, battle flags were hoisted and planes were prepared for a counterstrike. However, luck aboard the ship was to be no better that day than it had been for the scout bombers or would be for the planes landing at Pearl after dark. Without operational radar or organized air search, communications intercepted from various American ships and planes were more confusing than enlightening. Finally, interception of a Japanese radio transmission indicated the longitudinal bearing of the enemy. The decision aboard the carrier was to launch planes toward the southern end of the bearing, the wrong direction, with the consequence that *Enterprise* planes found only ships of their own navy. Admiral Morison in Volume Three of his *History of United States Naval Operations in World War II* concluded that this error, although a dis-

appointment to all aboard the carrier, was another blessing in disguise for *Enterprise* that day. *Enterprise*, already short the planes that had flown to Pearl Harbor, was at that time inadequately armed with only sixteen undependable 1.1" antiaircraft guns and a small number of .50-caliber machine guns and would have been challenging six enemy carriers with nearly 400 planes.

At the end of the day it was apparent the war had not started well for *Enterprise*. Her air groups had been hurt and perceptions aboard that evening were that nothing had gone right. But this was only the first of 1,364 days of war for the big carrier and the good fortune that kept *Enterprise* from being in Pearl and from finding an uneven fight on 7 December 1941 would continue with her throughout the war.

All day Monday 8 December *Enterprise* steamed off the entrance of Pearl Harbor awaiting the return of the Japanese. However, the six enemy fleet carriers (flagship *Akagi*, *Kaga*, *Hiryu*, *Soryu*, *Shokaku* and *Zuikaku*) were on their way west. *Hiryu* and *Soryu* would stop off at Wake Island to provide air support for the invasion there and then sail on to rejoin the fleet in Japan. On the evening of the 8th, *Enterprise* slipped into Pearl Harbor to refuel and take on supplies. Entering the harbor at dusk men aboard the carrier viewed the destruction of the previous day's battle: battleships *Arizona*, *Oklahoma*, *West Virginia* and *California* sunk or sinking; battleship *Nevada* aground; cruiser *Helena* badly damaged; and destroyers *Cassin*, *Downes* and *Shaw* shattered. Damage to land installations was clearly evident, and although death could not be seen it could be smelled and perceived by other senses. Aboard the carrier hearts hardened and resolve burned brighter than the flames still emanating from the *Arizona*.

The remaining days of December 1941 were spent by *Enterprise* patrolling back and forth off the coast of Hawaii. On 10 December an *Enterprise* plane dropped a bomb on a Japanese submarine (I-70) operating on the surface and thus provided the carrier with the distinction of destroying the first enemy combat ship of the war. However, this happy note was negated when word arrived on 23 December that Wake Island had fallen and the Marine pilots delivered to that island earlier in the month by the carrier were now either dead or captured.

When the historic year of 1941 closed, *Enterprise* was still on patrol and the new year was celebrated only by reaffirmation of resolutions to settle some scores with the Japanese. Settlement would not be long in coming. The year 1942 would be the year of the Big E.

THE TRAGEDY OF AIR GROUP 6

I was to be second-in-command of a flight of six F4F-4 fighters from the U.S.S. Enterprise that were to escort 19 torpedo planes and six scout planes on our way to find the Japanese Fleet, which a report said had been located.

Unfortunately, the report was erroneous, as we later found out. However, we were launched and went out some 200 miles.

It was dark when we returned to the ship and my flight leader talked to the Enterprise, and asked for permission to land. The ship said, "Hell, no. We're not going to light up for you. Go into Pearl Harbor," and gave us a coded direction.

We turned on the heading toward Pearl. Everything was blacked out except burning ships, which we thought were burning cane fields. It was 8:30 Sunday night.

As we passed Diamond Head we turned toward Ford Island in a loose formation and were given permission to land. Most of our gauges had been indicating we were running out of fuel for the last 20 minutes.

When we broke formation in preparation for landing, everything in Pearl Harbor opened up on us with their antiaircraft batteries. The sky was ablaze with gun tracers.

Lt. (j.g.) Fritz Hebel, the squadron commander, took off towards Wheeler Field but was shot down and killed when he tried to land. Ens. Herb Menges crashed and was killed at Pearl City. Ens. Gayle Hermann's plane took a 5-inch shell through his engine, and spun in right on the Ford Island golf course. He survived. Ens. David Flynn bailed out over Barbers Point and we found him 10 days later at Tripler Army Hospital with a broken leg. Ens. Eric Allen was killed by a .50-caliber machine gun bullet after parachuting from his crippled plane.

I called the Ford Island tower and told them I was coming in. I put my wheels down and headed back right over the harbor about 50 feet over the water.

I roared right past the foretop of the Nevada. They turned all their guns on me but nothing connected.

Moments later I touched the runway. I overshot. There were two crash trucks in front of me at the end of the runway. I slammed on the brakes and spun around in a full circle on the first green of a golf course just beyond the field.

I taxied back up the field. A Marine gunner sprayed the plane with bullets. He just missed my head.

Of the six planes and pilots I was the only one to land intact; three others were killed.

After this frightening experience, I went to the BOQ to find a bed. I could see and hear the Arizona still burning. I wanted to call my wife who was staying east of Pearl City but assumed that with all the damage around that there would be no telephone service. I picked up the phone anyway, and to my surprise got a dial tone. To my complete surprise I dialed my number and got through to my wife.

I was the luckiest man in the Navy on Dec. 7, 1941.

Capt. Jim Daniels, Ret.
Kailua, Hawaii

Enterprise off Pearl Harbor in 1940. Planes furthest aft are Douglas Devastator TBDs with BT-1 bombers ahead. Forward of the ship's island are the last biplane fighters to operate from American carriers.

USN

USS Oglala *sunk at Pearl Harbor 7 December 1941.* Oglala *was raised and served to the war's end. Had* Enterprise *been at Pearl as scheduled she, like* Oglala *and* Oklahoma *would have probably capsized to port.* NA

One of the classic pictures of the Pearl Harbor attack 7 December 1941. From left are battleships West Virginia, Tennessee *and* Arizona. Arizona *remains today where she sank,* Tennessee *sailed from Pearl within days of the attack and* West Virginia *was raised, repaired, modernized and returned to the Pacific to fight the last two years of the war.* NA

CHAPTER THREE
The Offensive Defensive: 1942-1943

The last month of 1941 and the first five months of 1942 were among the darkest in American history. For six months news reports brought the bad news of continuing defeats. In January the Japanese entered the South Asian country of Burma and Manila, the capital of the Philippines; in February they captured Singapore and invaded Java; in March the Dutch East Indies fell; in April the American and Philippine forces on Bataan capitulated; and in May the gallant remnant of the American and Philippine resistance on Corregidor struck the colors.

News from the European theater was equally discouraging and in these first months of the war the American attitude went through several changes. The presumptuous contempt of early December 1941 became disbelief on 7 December 1941, anger on 8 December, bravado on the 9th and doubt on the 10th and 11th when news arrived of the sinking of the two British capital ships, *Prince of Wales* and *Repulse*. From the end of December on, however, the tone and essence of the times was that of a quiet resolve.

While major attention centered on invasions and land battles, the role of the Japanese navy in support of these operations was not overlooked by American naval strategists. Even if the attack on Pearl Harbor had not occurred, the U.S. Navy would not have been strong enough in early 1942 to cross the Pacific in strength and challenge the Japanese. In both numbers and quality the enemy had an advantage. Cruiser strength was comparable and the two combatants were relatively close in other ship types. However, the paramount difference was in aircraft carriers, island-based aircraft and the natural defensive advantage of fighting on interior lines.

In the early months of the war Japan could place at sea six first-class fleet carriers and three light carriers. The United States could initially respond with only three fleet carriers. *Saratoga* was struck by a submarine torpedo early in January (12th) and would not return until summer. Filling the void left by *Saratoga* was *Yorktown*, hastily transferred from the Atlantic to join *Lexington* and *Enterprise. Hornet* would arrive in April to bring American strength to four, but *Lexington* would be lost in early May to again widen the gap of relative strength. Japanese

possession of Pacific island bases before the war and the quick occupation of others, including former U.S. possessions Wake Island and Guam, strengthened outer and inner defensive perimeters. Consequently, a quick American response was all but impossible and this explains the inability of American forces to reinforce and rescue their beleaguered colleagues in the Philippines. In the Pacific the gospel of war was, and would be, that one first had to have control of the air and control of the sea before one could expect success on land. Between January and May 1942 Japan had defeated the small United States, British and Dutch naval contingents in the Far East and by 1 May stood poised to extend their power southward to Australia and eastward to Midway.

Between January and May 1942 American naval responses to the Japanese surge were insignificant in retrospect, but at the time of their occurrence they were greatly hailed. *Enterprise* was present and involved in all the early swipes at the enemy and it was in these days that the ship began to acquire the sobriquet by which history would remember her...The Big E.

January 1942 was a month similar to December 1941 in that *Enterprise* was still operating in a defensive role. Even on 11 January when she left Hawaiian patrol duty to sail with a convoy ordered to reinforce Samoa, her role was defensive. That mission of protection complete, the ship was ready to begin the first assaults against the enemy.

In those first six months of the war the realities of the balance of sea power in the Pacific and the decision to assign priority to the European theater dictated a strategy of an "offensive defensive" for the Pacific theater. Time would be required to bring new ships and many more men to the area before a true offensive thrust could commence, but what was held by the allies in the central and southwestern Pacific had to be held lest the cost of reclaiming the strongholds be prohibitive. The loss of Midway in the central Pacific would threaten Pearl Harbor and Hawaii and further losses in the southwestern Pacific would mean the isolation of Australia wherein General MacArthur was planning the future allied push north through New Guinea, the western Solomons, the Philippines, and finally, Japan. So, it became the mission of *Enterprise, Lex-*

ington and *Yorktown* to occupy the thoughts of the Imperial Japanese Navy by striking outer perimeter bases on a north-south line. Great results in terms of material damage to the enemy were not expected, but it was expected that the upcoming raids would buy time for gathering strength, uplifting morale, and provide battle experience in anticipation of the day when the enemy would again offer challenge by a move south toward Australia or east toward Midway. But the more immediate need was to head off an expected push against Samoa which would most likely emanate from bases in the Marshall Islands. This strategy was founded on the belief that the Marshall Island bases had been the staging point for the successful assault against Wake Island.

On 1 February Admiral Halsey on *Enterprise* was in position to strike Kwajalein, Wotje, Roi and Maloeap while the *Yorktown* group to the south was poised to hit Jaluit, Mili, and Makin, the northernmost enemy base in the Gilbert Islands. Of the two strikes the *Enterprise* group was more successful. Although initial reports indicated numerous ships sunk at Kwajalein—including combat types—postwar evidence indicated only a transport and subchaser had actually been destroyed, but eight other ships had been damaged. About two dozen enemy planes and several installations were added to the day's total. The raid had been daring and dangerous as the *Enterprise* steamed well within range of enemy land-based planes and remained in a confined area long enough to invite a submarine attack. When enemy resistance came to the carrier early in the afternoon it was, fortunately, in the form of only a handful of planes. At least three of the attackers were shot down by *Enterprise's* CAP (combat air patrol) and gunfire from the carrier.

Ammunition hoists bringing bombs to the flight deck during the Marshall Islands raid, 1 February 1942.   USN

In the first air attack against Enterprise *during the February 1942 Marshall Islands raid .50-caliber machine guns were the "close-in" antiaircraft guns. Note the lack of headgear and life jackets in this early battle.* USN

TBDs and F4Fs spotted on flight deck of Enterprise *11 April 1942 on the way to the Halsey-Doolittle Tokyo raid.* USN

This first occasion under fire was memorable for reasons other than just being a first. The event called attention to the inadequacy of both the antiaircraft guns in use at the time (eight 5-inch-.25 caliber, sixteen 1.1-inch "Chicago Piano's," and numerous .50 caliber Browning machine guns) and the marksmanship of the gunners. Also, the attack was one of the first occasions American sailors would watch a Japanese pilot attempt to crash his plane against their ship. This attempt failed, but only by a matter of inches. The tail section of a parked plane was sheared off as the Japanese bomber struck the aft portion of the flight deck and crashed into the sea. A wing of the Japanese plane landed aboard the *Enterprise* and before the war was over at least two other wings from attacking enemy planes would also be deposited aboard the carrier. One of these wings still exists today, boxed away in storage at the U.S. Navy Museum storage facility in Williamsburg, Virginia.

The day of return to Pearl Harbor was occasion for considerable celebration. One would have thought the engagement in the Marshalls and Gilberts had won the war in one fell swoop. But the war was young and to that point there had been precious little to celebrate. Later in the year when *Enterprise* would twice return to Pearl with holes in her flight deck, hull plates reinforced by mattresses and timbers, and with gaping holes in her interior, the greetings would be infinitely more solemn and somber even though her victories in those battles would justify the noisy, ebullient demonstrations of early February.

Time in port was short. On 14 February *Enterprise* was at sea again, off this time to raid Wake Island. Earlier a task force built around *Saratoga* had headed for Wake, but turned back. Later, a task force built around *Lexington* headed for Wake but also aborted. This time, however, the raid would come off. Wake Island was indeed a meaningful target for the men of *Enterprise*. At least they would derive some satisfaction in striking at those who had been responsible for the death and capture of the men *Enterprise* had carried to the island three months earlier. In fact, little damage to the enemy was administered during the 24 February raid, and the raid on Marcus Island on 4 March was significant in retrospect only for its daring in that the island was only 1,000 miles from the Japanese homeland and for the use of radar to guide the carrier's planes to the target. Still, the efforts of these early raids brought considerable attention and respect to the ship within the Navy. The general public would hear the story of the raids, but the name of the ship or ships involved were seldom released until long after the event. Some stories about the *Enterprise* did reach the public, however. One of the first involved the story of three *Enterprise* aircrewmen who got lost during the Samoan convoy mission and were at sea for 34 days. Their ordeal and experiences were told to the public in R. Trumbull's *The Raft*.

Enterprise returned to Pearl in March and remained in port until April. During this time there was the usual replenishment of supplies and maintenance, but this time was also used to make minor alterations and repairs. The most significant alteration was the removal of most .50-caliber machine guns and the installation of the new 20mm Oerlikons. Again, post-war review would not give the Oerlikon terribly high marks, but at the time it was a big improvement over the .50-caliber Brownings. It is interesting to note, perhaps, that the post-war negative comments did not come from men aboard the *Enterprise* in 1942. Granted, one could watch the Oerlikons tracers begin to fall at a distance of 3,000 yards, but the spectacle of the gunfire from this weapon lifted American spirits and in the August 1942 Battle of the Eastern Solomons the gun would endear itself to men of the Big E as it would help account for 15 enemy planes on that day. The 20mm would be on board for the remainder of the war with its numbers ranging up to 60.

Most of the pictures of the carrier in this section were taken while the ship was in Pearl during late March, early April and late May 1942. One cannot help but wonder if the many pictures taken at this time from so many different perspectives and showing such detail were not taken with the thought in mind that the Navy had better assemble a pictorial record before the ship was lost in battle. Regardless, the pictures taken during this period are among the best of the over 500 official Navy pictures held today by the Navy and the National Archives. Comparison of the pictures in this section with those of later sections make apparent the numerous changes in the appearance of the ship during its operational life. The major alterations would occur in 1943 while in Bremerton for overhaul and comments are offered later on the changes made at that time.

At sea again the second week in April, the carrier headed northwest with the vast majority of officers and men not knowing their next destination and mission. On 13 April men aboard *Enterprise* got their first look at the Big E's new "stepsister," *Hornet* (CV-8). Whereas *Enterprise* and *Yorktown* had been authorized at the same time (1933), built and fitted out within sight of each other, *Hornet* was not authorized until 1938, was launched in 1940 and commissioned in 1941. She had been constructed on the same plan as *Enterprise* and *Yorktown* but there were minor differences in appearance. The chief differences were the more rounded contours of the bridge and a slightly different design at the top of the distinctive tripod mast. Ironically, the changes to *Enterprise* in 1943 would make the bridge of *Enterprise* resemble that of *Hornet,* but by that time there would be no mistaking the two ships because *Hornet* would die in only a little over four months from this April day which marked her entry into the combat arena.

On 13 April 1942, however, *Hornet* was very much alive. Although her own planes were stored away inside the ship's hangar deck, her flight deck was filled from the island aft with 16 U.S. Army Air Corps B-25s. Also aboard was Lt. Col. James H. "Jimmy" Doolittle and 79 volunteers who would man the B-25s for a surprise raid against the heart and capital of the enemy, Tokyo.

Soon after *Hornet* was sighted word was passed to the men of *Enterprise* regarding their destination and mission. Despite the obvious danger of sailing to within 500 miles of the Japanese coast with only *Enterprise* planes available for combat air patrol defense, launching the B-25s for their early evening raid and then trying to retire before enemy land-based planes and surface units could attack, morale within the carriers and attending ships soared. According to official reports and reminiscences, morale was sustained throughout the several days of the approach.

On 18 April a scout plane from *Enterprise* discovered an enemy patrol craft and was in turn discovered. The plane returned to the Big E and dropped a message of the sighting onto the flight deck. The problem was not the sighting; that was expected. What was not expected was the location: the American raiders were still 150 miles from the planned launching point. Within an hour an enemy patrol craft was sighted from the Big E and Admiral Halsey, commanding the operation from the bridge of *Enterprise,* ordered Colonel Doolittle to launch his planes immediately, and just as soon as the last B-25 lifted from the deck of *Hornet* the two carriers reversed track and headed for Pearl.

For the Japanese 18 April was a day of surprises. One of the patrol boats that spotted the two carriers was a bit late getting off a report to Tokyo because the sailor on watch had taken time to admire the beauty of the carriers which he believed to be Japanese. And the alerted headquarters in Tokyo believed the raid would not commence until the following morning since they expected navy planes which had a smaller flying range than the B-25s. Consequently, the altered time schedule did not adversely affect the success of the raid. The B-25s flew over Tokyo and other cities in broad daylight, dropped their few bombs and continued on toward China. Only nine of the 80 Army pilots and crew were lost. Surprise was all but total.

The announcement by President Roosevelt of the first successful attack against the Japanese homeland mentioned the role of the Army but not that of the Navy. Even though top enemy commanders knew the raid had come from carriers, the President suggested the starting point was the

The following photographs are of the Enterprise *at Pearl Harbor in May 1942. The new 20mm Oerlikons have replaced the .50-caliber Brownings. Note the 5-inch guns and 1.1 "Chicago Piano" antiaircraft guns and the relative paucity of radar installations compared to island appearance later in the war.* USN

mythical "Shangri La." Especially in the first year of the war secrecy was a critical factor because of limited American strength, and so it was that in the year 1942 *Enterprise* would receive little or no publicity concerning her role in this and subsequent triumphs and trials. By 1944 American naval strength was such that events were reported to the general public soon after they occurred and ships' identities were revealed whether the news was good or bad. And in 1944 when the full story of the Halsey-Doolittle raid was released to the public, details of the Navy's contribution were noted and rather quickly forgotten because of the flood of information concerning current battles and events.

History records the Tokyo raid as a stunt to build morale, which it did. But the raid also had military ramifications. Debate within the Japanese military circles in April had turned to the "what next?" stage as initial Japanese objectives in southeast Asia neared successful completion. The Army wanted to follow the long-held plan of holding fast and defending the empire from interior lines. But Admiral Yamamoto, the architect of the Pearl Harbor raid, wanted to draw the American fleet into decisive

battle before the industrial strength of the United States could become a factor. The Tokyo raid brought debate to a halt. The sacred soil of Japan had been molested and the American carrier force and its bases had to be destroyed. Therefore, plans for the invasion of Midway were hastily drawn and the Imperial Japanese Navy prepared for an offensive that was sure to draw the American Fleet to sea in defense of their island base only 1,300 miles from Hawaii.

Entry at Pearl on 25 April was again a moment to remember for men aboard *Enterprise,* and the moment was especially rewarding for the crew of *Hornet:* her first test had been passed with considerable distinction. But there would be no time for celebration. One major component of the Japanese Fleet was already at sea heading toward the Coral Sea and Australia while another was gathering ships for the push on Midway.

The period of the "offensive defensive" was over. The next two engagements were strictly defensive for the U.S. Navy and the responsibility for defense would fall upon carriers *Enterprise,* sister ship *Yorktown*, stepsister *Hornet* and *Lexington.*

Enterprise *at Pearl Harbor in May 1942.*

Enterprise *at Pearl Harbor in May 1942.*

USN

Enterprise *planes preparing for launch 4 May 1942 while en route to the Battle of the Coral Sea.* Enter-prise *arrived one day too late to fight; this was the only major Pacific battle the Big E would miss during the war.*

USN

CHAPTER FOUR
Coral Sea and Midway:
The First Two Fleet Carrier Battles

From 25 April, the day of return from the Tokyo raid, until 30 April 1942 work proceeded furiously to prepare *Enterprise* and *Hornet* for their next mission. Battle was coming somewhere along the approaches to Australia and the hope was that the Big E and *Hornet* could join *Yorktown* and *Lexington* in time for what would be the first of six major battles between Japanese and United States fleet carriers. On 30 April *Enterprise* and *Hornet* departed Pearl for the 3,500-mile voyage to the Coral Sea.

For the second time in the young war fate would turn a blind eye toward *Enterprise* as she sought to close with and do battle against enemy carriers. Whereas a turn in the wrong direction precluded battle on 7 December 1941, timing would be the culprit this first week of May 1942. Distance was too great and *Enterprise* would miss by one day the battle of the Coral Sea. It was to be the only major Pacific sea battle she would miss during the entire war.

In the Coral Sea fight the Japanese had lost the light carrier *Shoho*, and fleet carrier *Shokaku* had been badly damaged. *Shokaku's* sister ship *Zuikaku* had escaped injury but sustained serious aircrew losses. Consequently two of the enemy Pearl Harbor raiders, *Sho* and *Zui,* would not be available for the forthcoming Midway battle. This fact was perhaps more significant to American fortunes than the fact that the enemy invasion force had turned back during the Coral Sea conflict. Port Moresby and the route to Australia had been successfully defended, but the cost was high. *Lexington* CV-2, at the time one of the largest warships in the world and upon whose deck many of *Enterprise's* pilots had trained, was lost. *Lex* had taken three bomb hits and two torpedoes and although able to steam away from the battle site her doom was sealed by inadequate damage control. Internal explosions required her abandonment and she was scuttled by her own escorts on 8 May. Her loss was keenly felt on *Enterprise* and was particularly felt at Pearl where Admiral Nimitz was formulating plans to meet the Midway assault. Not only was *Lexington* gone, but *Yorktown* had been badly damaged by an enemy bomb and was limping back to Pearl.

American cryptanalysts had broken the Japanese code and therefore knew the enemy plan. An invasion force to occupy Midway would be supported by battleships and smaller units of the enemy fleet. And leading the procession of Japanese naval might across the Pacific would be four veterans of the Pearl Harbor attack, carriers *Akagi* (again the flagship), *Kaga, Soryu* and *Hiryu*.

In the nearly six months since their success at Pearl Harbor the four enemy carriers had enjoyed other triumphs. *Soryu* and *Hiryu* had supported the attack and invasion of Wake Island, and there is little question that the success of that venture rested with the air support provided by the two carriers. *Akagi, Hiryu* and *Soryu* had combined talents to sink the 11,000-ton British light-carrier *Hermes*— the world's first aircraft carrier designed, ordered and built to be such—in the Indian Ocean on 9 April. And all four carriers contributed to the defeat of allied land forces throughout southeast Asia by providing air support, sinking allied warships and closing shipping lanes. Not only were they undefeated but they had yet to be significantly challenged.

To meet the oncoming Japanese fleet Admiral Nimitz sent his only three operational carriers in the Pacific to a point northeast of Midway. This would be the only time the three sister ships— *Enterprise, Yorktown* and *Hornet*—would operate together, but this one occasion would be memorable.

Although the performance of the sister ships would in the end make the battle of Midway memorable, sentiment prior to the battle was not terribly positive. United States naval strength to stop the enemy threat was not impressive in relative terms. The Japanese had more ships, bigger ships, more battle tested crewmen and more carriers. The American answer included no battleships, fewer ships of all types and only three carriers which included one with no direct battle experience (*Hornet*), one of questionable readiness due to battle damage (*Yorktown*), and *Enterprise,* "the best of our carriers, with a seasoned air group" according to Admiral Morison. (pg. 82, Vol. IV)

The battle broke on 4 June when enemy carrier planes struck an alert and well-fortified Midway Island. At the conclusion of the attack Lt. Joichi Tomonaga, commander of the *Hiryu* air group, radioed Admiral Nagumo aboard flagship *Akagi* that the runways at Midway were still intact and that

Enterprise en route to the Battle of Midway June 1942. Only four of the TBD Devastators of the squadron shown in this picture survived the battle. NA

American defenders on the island were still quite active. Lt. Tomonaga's recommendation for another strike against the island was given support in the thinking of Admiral Nagumo as he watched American Army and Navy land-based planes launch torpedoes and drop bombs on his formation. Although no hits were registered against the Japanese ships in these first attacks, Nagumo accepted the recommendation of Tomonaga and Commander Minoru Genda, tactical planner for Pearl Harbor and this battle, to strike Midway a second time.

Japanese planes ready to be launched at that moment were armed with bombs and torpodoes designed to attack American ships, as yet unseen but expected. The order was given to change to bombs designed for land targets and the process began. The time required for the change would allow the first strike planes to return, land, refuel, rearm and be ready for a third strike against Midway or be ready to meet the expected challenge at sea. An hour after this order was given, the Japanese Admiral received first word from one of his scout planes that an American carrier (*Yorktown*) was within two hours flying time of his ships. However, Nagumo could not react instantly because the planes aboard his carriers were still rearming and he was in the process of recovering other planes from the first strike. Three-quarters of an hour later recovery was complete, but time had passed for the Japanese fleet to take further offensive action. American carrier planes were on the horizon.

At 9:30 on the morning of 4 June 1942 the Rising Sun of Japan reached its zenith. By 10:30 that same morning the Rising Sun began to set.

Planes from Task Force 16, *Enterprise* and *Hornet,* should have arrived over the Japanese carriers together, but enroute *Hornet's* bombers and fighters did not find the enemy at the expected position, turned to search toward Midway and thereby missed the day's fight. *Hornet's* torpedo planes did find the enemy, however, and they, along with the torpedo squadrons from *Enterprise* and *Yorktown* made their heroic attack. Of the 41 Douglas Devastator TBDs representing the three American carriers only four returned to *Enterprise*, two to *Yorktown* and none returned to *Hornet.* Capable of only 125 knots when armed, the obsolete Devastators were no match for the fast Japanese fighters and hundreds of enemy antiaircraft guns.

The sacrifice of the Devastators was not in vain. Attention of enemy ship's gunners and enemy combat air patrol was directed to the Devastators operational area which was approximately 50 feet above sea level. Without notice, high above the uneven battle appeared nearly 40 SBD Douglas Dauntless dive-bombers from *Enterprise*. These planes, like those from the *Hornet,* had arrived at a point in the ocean where the enemy ships should have been. Not finding them there, Lt. Commander Clarence Wade McClusky chose to fly north—the bearing opposite Midway—and continue his search beyond the safe range of his fuel. Less than half an hour later he was above the enemy carriers and in position to change the character of the Pacific war.

Commander McClusky ordered Lt. Earl Gallaher and his planes to follow him down to drop their bombs on *Kaga* and directed Lt. Dick Best to lead his planes down to attack *Akagi.* Two or three bombs struck *Akagi,* four struck *Kaga.* The destructive force of the bombs was greatly supplemented by the exploding bombs and fuel within the just-refueled and rearmed Japanese planes. The eruptions were cataclysmic. What had been two proud, powerful floating machines of war were in minutes humbled, shattered, sinking wrecks.

Fate had finally introduced *Enterprise* to the enemy carriers she had hungered to meet for six very long months.

At the same time McClusky, Gallaher and Best were diving on *Akagi* and *Kaga,* SBDs from *Yorktown* were diving on *Soryu.* The *Yorktown* dive-bombers had started later than those from *Enterprise* and *Hornet* but could not have timed their arrival at any more favorable moment. *Soryu* was struck by three bombs and left a flaming derelict. Shortly after, the enemy carrier was hit by torpedoes fired by submarine USS *Nautilus. Soryu* burned, broke up and sank just before dark.

While *Enterprise* and *Yorktown* SBDs were raining death upon *Akagi, Kaga* and *Soryu,* the fourth Japanese carrier, *Hiryu,* sailed on untouched. As American planes returned to *Yorktown* and *Enterprise,* torpedo planes and bombers rose from the deck of *Hiryu* in an attempt to reverse the tide of battle. By following the American planes, the Japanese found the closest American carrier, *Yorktown,* and began their attack.

Of the three American carriers it was unfortunate that enemy planes found *Yorktown* instead of the *Enterprise-Hornet* task force which was only 10 to 15 miles away. *Yorktown* had been so often at sea since entering the Pacific there had been no time to replace all the .50-caliber machine guns with 20mm Oerlikens. Also, *Yorktown* was operating alone and therefore had fewer combat air patrol planes to cover her, and a number of these were being refueled when enemy bombers arrived. Despite an admirable performance by *Yorktown's* combat air patrol, several bombers got through and scored three hits which slowed the ship and later brought her to a stop. In little over an hour the carrier was moving again, but slowly. The refueling of her Wildcat fighters for defense was disrupted by the need to drain fuel lines while under attack. Consequently, only 12 fighters were able to meet the incoming second attack.

The second attack from *Hiryu* was led by the same officer who had broadcast the need for the followup strike on Midway earlier in the day, Lt. Tomonaga. Just as Tomonaga's planes appeared in

Enterprise *during the Battle of Midway 4 June 1942.*

NA

Akagi, *the Japanese flagship at both Pearl Harbor and Midway, sunk at Midway by* Enterprise *dive-bombers.*   USN

Kaga, *shown at sea in 1936, was also sunk at Midway by* Enterprise *dive-bombers.*   USN

Hiryu *on trials 28 April 1939.* Hiryu *died under bombs from* Enterprise *and* Yorktown *SBDs flying from the deck of* Enterprise *after* Yorktown *was disabled 4 June 1942.*   USN

Soryu *underway in 1938.* Soryu *was sunk by* Yorktown *SBDs led by Lt. Commander Max Leslie who would command a squadron aboard* Enterprise *later in 1942 during the Guadalcanal struggle.*   USN

Hiryu *burning on the morning of 5 June 1942. Photographs were taken from a Japanese plane.*   USN

the distance, Lt. John Adams was preparing to fly his Wildcat fighter down *Yorktown's* hastily patched deck. With only a few gallons of fuel in his tanks Adams lifted off *Yorktown* attempting to charge his guns, turn a crank to retract his wheels, dodge the gunfire from "friendly" ships, and intercept the enemy torpedo planes. He was successful in shooting down one of the torpedo planes, perhaps the plane in which Lt. Tomonaga died, but to this day (1982) he cannot remember whether or not the enemy plane had already dropped its torpedo. Despite Adam's effort and that of other fighter pilots and ship's gunners, two torpedoes struck the port side of *Yorktown* and she quickly heeled over to a 26-degree list.

With *Yorktown* now mortally wounded and *Hornet* without planes (torpedo planes shot down; bombers and fighters at Midway) only *Enterprise* was left to continue the battle. The situation was simple: *Enterprise* against *Hiryu*.

As the few Japanese planes to survive the attack on *Yorktown* departed, homeless *Yorktown* SBDs and Wildcats (including Lt. John Adams) landed aboard *Enterprise*. Hastily two dozen SBDs representing both *Enterprise* and *Yorktown* squadrons were armed, fueled and sent off without fighter escort for reprisal against *Hiryu*. Just before sundown this flight, led by the Big E's Earl Gallaher who was substituting for the wounded McClusky, found *Hiryu* as she was preparing to launch her planes and

Lt. Joichi Tomonaga, Imperial Japanese Navy. Tomonaga radioed the report from Midway recommending a second strike and was the commander of the torpedo attack on Yorktown *during which he was killed.* USN

the events of the morning were repeated again. Four large bombs tore gaping holes in *Hiryu's* flight deck and damaged her beyond repair. She would stay afloat until the following morning, long enough for a Japanese pilot to take the pictures that appear herein, and then she joined *Akagi, Kaga* and *Soryu* at the bottom of the Pacific.

The carrier battle was completed by sundown 4 June, but the several Japanese naval groups in the vicinity attempted several probes to bait the American carriers either into a night surface action or into range of Japanese land-based planes on Wake. Admiral Raymond Spruance, Task Force 16 commander aboard flagship *Enterprise,* had received tactical freedom from senior commander Admiral Frank Jack Fletcher (Task Force 17) when Fletcher's flagship, *Yorktown,* was abandoned. Spruance, normally a cruiser commander, was well versed in surface tactics and strategy and he recognized the enemy baiting tactics for what they were. However, he did maneuver his two carriers in position for further opportunities to strike the enemy. Early on 6 June his strategy was rewarded with the discovery of two enemy heavy cruisers, *Mogami* and *Mikuma,* and attending destroyers. Planes from the Big E and *Hornet* sank *Mikuma* and seriously damaged *Mogami* and a destroyer. With this action the battle of Midway closed although the opposing forces did not break contact until 11 June.

Celebration of the great victory was muted when *Enterprise* returned to Pearl on 13 June because too many of her aircrew members had been lost and because the Big E had lost her identical twin, *Yorktown.* Prematurely abandoned on the 4th and re-entered on the 6th it appeared for a time the courageous carrier could be saved. However, two more torpedoes, fired from an enemy submarine, struck the carrier and a third hit attending destroyer *Hammann* on the afternoon of the 6th. *Hammann* sank in less than five minutes. *Yorktown* fought death until the morning of the 7th at which time she passed from sight.

For Admiral Fletcher the loss of *Yorktown* was an especially sad moment. Only 30 days earlier he had lost another flagship, *Lexington.*

For Lt. John Adams it was a doubly sad moment. It was bad enough that he had to accept the loss of his ship. Forty years afterward he still anguishes over the lack of fuel that kept him and his fellow fighter pilots from adequately defending *Yorktown* against the final attack. And he still anguishes over the fate of *Hammann.* On one occasion that destroyer had fished him out of the Pacific when his plane did not make it back to *Yorktown,* and the day before the Coral Sea battle began *Hammann* plucked a fellow pilot and himself from the south coast of Guadalcanal after a forced landing.

Unquestionably, Midway was the turning point in the war. The United States did not win the war those early days of June 1942, but parity was achieved. The offensive thrust of Japan ended with this battle. From the middle of June 1942 until the end of the war Japan would find herself on the defensive.

At the time of the battle, news accounts were distorted by official censorship and by sketchy details. Throughout the war accounts were written and accepted as fact until post-war investigation and documents presenting the Japanese perspective brought history into a more proper focus. For these reasons *Enterprise* received little or no credit in the eyes of the general public for her contribution in this most significant naval battle of the war. But the fact is that the Big E had destroyed *Akagi* and *Kaga* on the morning of the historic 4th, and, when the battle was reduced to just *Enterprise* and *Hiryu* that afternoon, only *Enterprise* lived to see the afternoon of the following day.

Yorktown, *twin-sister of* Enterprise, *listing heavily to port after air attack on 4 June 1942. Struck by two submarine torpedoes against her starboard side on 6 June, the valiant carrier sank on 7 June.*   NA

Enterprise, *victor of Midway, at Pearl Harbor 12 July 1942. Note torpedo nets and camouflaged buildings on Ford Island.*
USN

CHAPTER FIVE
Eastern Solomons and Santa Cruz: Fleet Carrier Battles Three and Four

After Midway there was a five-week period in port for *Enterprise*. Little of the time, however, would be spent relishing the great victory of early June; there was simply too much to do. And the men privileged to do the celebrating, the survivors of the air battles at Midway, were being transferred. Most would return to the United States to help train the many new pilots needed for what was now recognized as a protracted conflict.

After a month of maintenance, replacement of aircrews, replenishment of planes, addition of a few crewmembers and a change in leadership on the bridge, *Enterprise* left Pearl on 15 July for the south Pacific. It would be three weeks before word would come from Admiral Thomas C. Kincaid and Captain Arthur C. Davis, the new commanding officers aboard, that the next mission for the Big E would be to support the landing of Marines on one of the easternmost islands of the Solomons...Guadalcanal.

OCCUPATION OF GUADALCANAL

In the early summer of 1942 Guadalcanal was at the easternmost extent of Japanese land-based air power and at the westernmost extent of American land-based air power. Planes from Rabaul, the Japanese stronghold on New Britain, could make their presence felt in the southeastern Solomons and American land-based planes from Espiritu Santo and New Caledonia could also overfly the area. Neither side, however, could control the southeastern Solomons without establishing there a permanent, defensible air base. This the Japanese began to do in late June 1942. This the United States could not tolerate. Although American strategic planners had considered a thrust up the Solomons to strengthen the United States-Australian defense line and to aid General MacArthur's planned northward thrust, it was the Japanese initiative in breaking ground for an airstrip on Guadalcanal that converted planning into action.

The battle for Guadalcanal began on 7 August 1942 exactly eight months to the day after the opening of the war. In a sense this battle would mark the true opening of the war. For the first time the two antagonists would meet at a point in the Pacific wherein neither had an advantage and where both could support the contest. Indeed, the purpose of this struggle would be to determine who would gain the advantage that would eventually culminate in victory.

The battle for Guadalcanal was a six-month battle in which the fortunes of war changed rapidly and radically for both Japanese and American forces. During the first three months of the campaign the issue was in doubt, and it was understood by all concerned that the navy which could wrest control of the waters around Guadalcanal would then control the air and the ground.

It is only conjecture, of course, what direction the Pacific war would have taken if *Enterprise* and *Hornet* had been lost with *Yorktown* at Midway and if *Akagi, Kaga, Soryu* and *Hiryu* had survived that battle. However, the United States undoubtedly would not have been able to think about *any* of the Solomon islands. Instead, American forces would have been digging in to defend Fiji, Samoa, New Caledonia and Hawaii and it is not unreasonable to believe that the bulk of the U.S. Pacific fleet might have been moved all the way back to the west coast. But, a relative degree of parity had been achieved by the results at Midway and for the first time in the war the Imperial Japanese Navy and the United States Navy could and would meet on fairly equal terms. In August 1942 the United States could count four fleet carriers in the Pacific (*Enterprise, Wasp, Saratoga* and *Hornet*) who together could operate approximately 300 planes while Japan could counter with two fleet carriers (*Shokaku* and *Zuikaku*) and five light carriers that combined could also operate approximately 300 planes. And to top things off, the first three new modern battleships were ready for service. USS *North Carolina* (BB-55) was already in the Pacific in August and her sister ship USS *Washington* (BB-56) and the USS *South Dakota* (BB-57) were preparing to pass through the Panama Canal within a matter of weeks.

The approach to Guadalcanal was the most impressive procession of American naval power yet assembled in the war. To *Enterprise* veterans who were accustomed to dashing into and out of enemy-controlled waters, the sight before them on 6 August was inspiring. Fourteen cruisers and the 35,000 ton battleship *North Carolina* were in view and their support of the Big E, *Saratoga* and *Wasp* boded well for an endeavor obviously shaping up to be more than a raid.

Although the days of raid-and-run were over, the new assignment of invasion support and cover was sufficiently dangerous to cause equal operational concern aboard the three carriers. Being restricted to a relatively small area to support an amphibious landing placed the carriers in constant peril from submarines as well as land-based aircraft. Too, this landing would not go unchallenged by enemy carrier-borne planes. The only question was when these perils would be encountered.

The first hours of the landings on 7 August went quite well for the Americans. *Enterprise* began the day before dawn with her air groups delivering bombing and strafing runs against both Guadalcanal and Tulagi, a seaplane base only 20 miles across the sound. The air groups of *Enterprise*, headed by Commander John Crommelin (who Commander Stafford would identify in his book *The Big E* as being the one man whose personality most indelibly stamped itself on the ship) and including Lt. Commander Max Leslie, who had led *Yorktown's* successful dive bombing attack against *Soryu* at Midway, set a combat record for one day by accomplishing 236 take-offs and 229 landings.

Later in the war (Iwo Jima 1945) *Enterprise* would set another record of more monumental proportions in support of the Marines but this first occasion's contribution would never be exceeded in importance.

Early in the afternoon of the 7th the first enemy land-based planes arrived to oppose the landings, but the F4F Wildcat fighters were equal to the task and the landing of troops and unloading of supplies was barely interrupted. On the 8th activities continued as they had the day previous. More enemy planes arrived to do battle, among them the most famous Japanese fighter pilot to survive the war—Saburo Sakai—who on this date was critically wounded by rearseat gunfire from the U.S. Navy's newest torpedo-bomber, the TBF Avenger.

By the evening of the 8th it was apparent that the landings had been a success and that American forces had gained the upper hand. After severe fighting at Tulagi, all Japanese defenders were dead and the lightly-defended, half-completed new airstrip on Guadalcanal was in American possession. The field was given the name Henderson Field in honor of the Marine major, Lofton Henderson, who was lost while defending another airstrip...Midway.

Enterprise crewmen prepare a plane for one of the record 236 takeoffs on the first day of the Guadalcanal invasion 7 August 1942.

NA

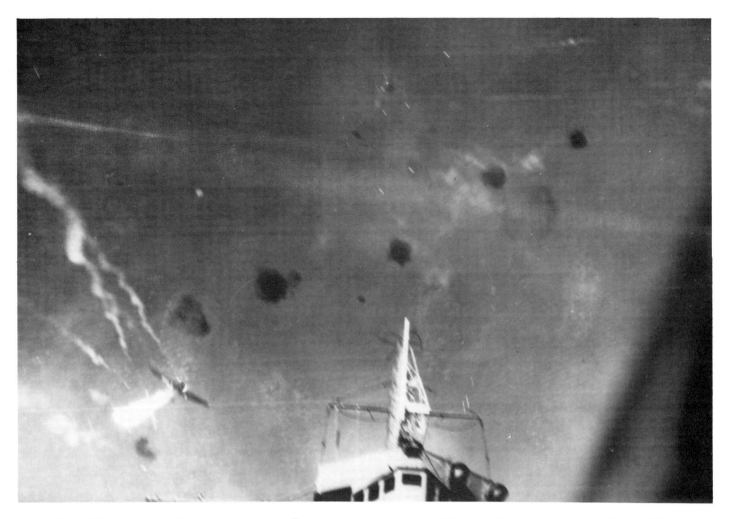

One of the Japanese planes shot down by Enterprise *gunners nearly falls onto the carrier. It crashed just off the port bow.*   NA

If one man was destined to have continual bad luck during the war on the allied side, that man must have been Admiral Frank Jack Fletcher. Fletcher, aboard *Saratoga,* a ship destined to endure more than her share of bad luck, had lost two previous flagships (*Lexington* and *Yorktown*) and his wartime fortunes were little better during the Solomons campaign. On the evening of the 8th Fletcher decided to remove the three American carriers from the immediate area of the landings thinking—with reasonable logic—the carriers would be safer if moved south. Unfortunately and unknown to the American admiral, a flotilla of seven Japanese cruisers and one destroyer was heading southeast from Rabaul to attack the American transports, newly landed troops and Henderson Field. Time of arrival was to be just after midnight and in the early morning darkness of 9 August the enemy ships surprised the American and Australian cruisers and destroyers guarding the landing site and left four cruisers sinking into what would become in name and fact "Ironbottom Sound." The disastrous battle of Savo Island, the first of several engagements between surface units in the struggle for Guadalcanal, immediately changed the strategic picture. For the next three months the Japanese would control the water around Guadalcanal at night while the United States would exert control during the day because of a slight advantage in the air thanks to the American aircraft carriers and the possession of Henderson Field.

The optimism of 6, 7 and 8 August quickly degenerated on the morning of the 9th as news of the Savo debacle spread, and half-loaded transports fled. Reason for the disconcerted American attitude was justified, not only because of what had just happened but also because the Japanese were in the process of transporting reinforcements to Guadalcanal—a project initially not too difficult in view of their nighttime nautical advantage. Further, the Japanese were organizing their carrier fleet for a major challenge to the American carriers with the ultimate goal of total control of Solomons' waters and the consequent reward of isolating American forces ashore.

The third bomb explosion on the Enterprise during the Battle of the Eastern Solomons. Note the continuing fire in the 5-inch gun gallery.   NA

The instant death for 38 Enterprise crewmen at the number three 5-inch gun gallery. Another bomb struck the same area moments earlier killing another 35.   NA

The hole in the flight deck caused by the third bomb to hit Enterprise *was patched over in an hour.*   NA

Enterprise *on the way to Pearl Harbor for repairs to Eastern Solomons battle damage. Note hull damage and pumps under damaged gun gallery. Large holes also existed below the waterline.*   NA

BATTLE OF THE EASTERN SOLOMONS

The expected sea challenge began on 23 August when the Japanese departed Truk and Rabaul with three carriers (*Shokaku*, *Zuikaku* and *Ryujo*), three battleships and a host of cruisers and destroyers to support the transports which would land reinforcements. For the Japanese the battle of the Eastern Solomons, sometimes referred to as the battle of the Stewart Islands, had begun. His bad luck holding, Admiral Fletcher detached *Wasp* and her supporting ships to fuel the next day (24th) therefore removing that carrier and her planes from the impending battle. And when news reached the admiral that the Japanese fleet was at sea, he again fell for the same tactics used by the enemy in the Coral Sea battle.

The enemy plan was to send forward light carrier *Ryujo*, just like her sister ship *Shoho* at Coral Sea, to draw American attention while the big fleet carriers *Shokaku* and *Zuikaku* steamed behind in order to strike the American carriers from ambush. The trap was sprung and it worked; only a lack of implementation, luck and some good shooting on the American side foiled the plan.

The coming of *Ryujo* on the 24th was known aboard *Enterprise* and *Saratoga* because she had been sighted by several scout planes. Two *Enterprise* SBDs attacked *Ryujo* after radioing her position but their bombs just missed. Not long after in that early afternoon *Enterprise* scout planes also found the real threat, *Shokaku* and *Zuikaku*. They attacked and recorded near misses on *Shokaku* and radioed the enemy carriers' position. However, bad communications prevented Admiral Fletcher from ordering planes from his flagship, *Saratoga*, to strike *Shokaku* and *Zuikaku* instead of *Ryujo*. The *Saratoga* strike against *Ryujo* was successful both from the Japanese and American point of view. The enemy trap with *Ryujo* as the lure had worked, and *Saratoga* enjoyed the highpoint of her wartime career as she pounded the enemy light carrier into her watery grave.

The report from *Enterprise* scouts concerning the presence of *Shokaku* and *Zuikaku* was soon confirmed by radar and later by sightings again as approximately 60 planes from the two big enemy carriers approached. *Saratoga's* luck held on this most significant day of her life and she was not attacked. *Enterprise* was to be the target of enemy wrath.

Because most of *Saratoga's* planes had taken the bait and attacked *Ryujo*, Admiral Fletcher ordered *Enterprise* to assume responsibility for combat air patrol direction. Admiral Fletcher, *Saratoga* and *Enterprise* were ready for the onslaught as over 50 Wildcat fighters were in place to greet the enemy bombers, torpedo planes and their escorting Zero fighters. Aboard *Enterprise*, Commander Crom-

melin suggested to Admiral Kincaid that the remaining 18 Avengers and SBDs be flown off. Most historical accounts refer to this incident as only a minor force flying off to engage the enemy, but to John Crommelin (who would retire as a Rear Admiral in 1950) this deck clearing flight most likely saved the carrier because the bombs that struck *Enterprise* later that day landed in the deck park area where these fueled and armed planes would have been.

With the sun dropping rapidly in the western sky the air battle above the American ships was joined. For Wildcat fighters of the combat air patrol and returning bombers and torpedo-bombers it was a banner day as enemy planes began falling from the sky. Still, the Japanese formation pressed on and gunfire from the Big E's antiaircraft batteries indicated the fact that approximately 30 enemy dive bombers had made it through the CAP and were now diving on the carrier. After the battle *Enterprise* would claim the downing of 44 enemy planes, 29 in aerial battles and 15 by the carrier's antiaircraft guns. However, the enemy would also make claims after the battle and although the carrier did not honor the claim to having been sunk, the claim of damage to *Enterprise* was fact.

The first bomb ever to strike *Enterprise* penetrated the flight deck at the edge of the number three (rear) elevator and tore downward several decks. The explosion killed 35 men, started fires, did considerable structural damage and punched several good-sized holes in the starboard quarter both above and below the water line. Only seconds later a second bomb struck within 15 feet of the first bomb and 38 men died instantly as the bomb and ignited powder in the number three 5-inch gun gallery exploded. The third and last bomb to hit the carrier landed on the aft portion of the number two (amidships) elevator just behind the island structure.

Of all the pictures taken in the Pacific theater during World War Two the ones taken during the five minutes *Enterprise* was under attack in this battle rank among the best and the most dramatic. *Life* magazine presented 22 pictures taken by a U.S. navy newsreel camera aboard *Enterprise* and printed them in the 14 December 1942 issue. Of course, *Enterprise* was not identified by name; at this point in the war national security could allow her to be identified only as "an unnamed U.S. aircraft carrier." The pictures in *Life* show the sequence of all three bomb hits. They depict several crewmembers dashing onto the flight deck from cover after the first two hits, turning to retreat for cover when the third bomb was spotted coming down, turning to look over the shoulder one last time and then disappearing when the last bomb exploded. Only those pictures available from the U.S. Navy and National Archives are presented here, but for the reader who will seek out the 14 December

1942 issue of *Life* for its sequence, it will be noted that one of the men in frame 10 lost an arm in the last explosion and that the severed arm struck another crewmember standing next to the camera recording the pictures.

The duel between the Japanese dive bombers and the gunners of *Enterprise* ended as quickly as it began. The Japanese planes still faced danger as they attempted once again to escape the combat air patrol, and *Enterprise*, too, still faced danger. Bright flames and clouds of smoke poured from the carrier, enough so that one can excuse the departing enemy airmen for reporting *Enterprise in extremis*. However, in less than an hour the major fires were out, repairs were begun on the perforated hull, the holes in the flight deck plated over and just before sunset, the still fast-moving carrier was receiving portions of her air group back aboard. Despite damage and death, things were looking up.

It is no wonder that the general demeanor of sailors was relatively matter-of-fact as the war expanded in time. In the Coral Sea *Lexington* was apparently out of danger when a series of unexpected, and avoidable explosions caused her loss, and

there was much reason for optimism that *Yorktown* could be saved just before she was hit by submarine torpedoes near Midway. And now it was the Big E's turn. While the last few planes were attempting to come aboard, the carrier's rudder jammed, the breakdown flag was raised, the carrier went into a circling pattern to starboard, an escorting destroyer was nearly run over, and radar indicated another 30 enemy planes were enroute. Fortunately, the Japanese second strike took a page from *Hornet's* book during the Midway fight, made a wrong turn, and did not find *Enterprise* in her impaired condition. And the steering problem was corrected in little over half an hour by an intrepid crewmember who crawled into a super-heated steering engine room to engage a motor. His brave act was only one of several that afternoon wherein crewmembers acting as individuals or well-trained groups saw trouble and disdained danger to do what was necessary to save their floating home. Despite the heroics of pilots and gunners, the mantle of distinction of 24 August 1942 went to the men of damage control—those who were on damage control duty and those who were self-appointed.

Damaged gun gallery and buckled flight deck.

NA

On the night of the 24th Admiral Fletcher ordered *Enterprise, Saratoga* and escorting ships south to avoid a night engagement. Except for some probing by both sides the battle was over. Strategically, victory went to the United States because the Japanese were not able to take control of the seas around Guadalcanal and land their troops by day: they would have to continue to bring in troops and supplies at night. Tactically, the victory also went to the United States. Japan had lost *Ryujo* and had lost the heart of her striking power from the decks of *Shokaku* and *Zuikaku* while *Enter-prise* and *Saratoga* lost fewer than 20 planes between them.

On the 25th *Enterprise* buried the 74 men killed during the previous day's bombing and the five who subsequently died of their wounds during the night. Also that day most of the Big E's planes were flown off to augment the Marine squadron at Henderson Field, and then the carrier turned toward Pearl Harbor for an appointment with the navy yard to repair her serious injuries. The third fleet-carrier battle of the war was history.

Hangar deck bulge before repairs at Pearl Harbor.　　　　　　NA

Damage to hull.　　　　　　USN

BATTLE OF SANTA CRUZ

While *Enterprise* was sailing to Pearl Harbor the Japanese fleet engaged in the Eastern Solomons battle was returning to Truk. There was no question there would be a return engagment. The Japanese would hurry to assemble at least three more light carriers and replace depleted aircrews aboard undamaged *Shokaku* and *Zuikaku.* At the earliest favorable moment the Japanese planned to return to Guadalcanal in force and accomplish the mission that had just failed.

Enterprise arrived at Pearl on 10 September and was under repair day and night until 16 October. A sign placed on the drydock informed one and all that this ship had first priority and accordingly navy yard personnel, civilian contractors and *Enterprise* crewmembers set about to bind the wounds of 24 August. Early on, some *Enterprise* crewmembers wondered aloud about the seemingly unenthusiastic attitude of some civilian workers. Closer investigation revealed, however, that the civilians were living a life of nothing but work and housing was so scarce at this time that three men had to share one bed in eight-hour shifts. But the work completed by the civilians was well-done and their cooperation was beyond reproach.

The news from Guadalcanal was mostly encouraging in that the Marines still held onto Henderson Field. News concerning the nocturnal surface actions around the contested island resembled a broken record: victory, defeat, victory, defeat, etc. On the high seas of the south Pacific the news was consistent, and it was bad. On 31 August *Saratoga* took her second torpedo within nine months from an enemy submarine and she would be lost to the fleet for three months. In 1942 the loss or unavailability of a carrier for any length of time was a crisis and *Saratoga* had missed Coral Sea and Midway due to the torpedo of 12 January; now she would miss the upcoming Battle of Santa Cruz and the Naval Battle of Guadalcanal. Worse was the news concerning *Wasp.* On 15 September she was hit by three submarine torpedoes and burned so severely that she had to be sunk by her escort. And within minutes of the time *Wasp* was struck the big battle-wagon *North Carolina* was hit by a torpedo and she too would miss the critical battles only a few weeks away. So, by the evening of 15 September only *Hornet,* the newest and least experienced American fleet-carrier, was left in the Solomon's area.

The news of the loss of *Wasp* threw work crews at Pearl into a higher gear as they rushed to complete work on *Enterprise.* Eagerness for return to the Solomons was so great that many of the items generally removed from a carrier about to enter dry-dock were left on board. In this instance ammunition, bombs and torpedoes were aboard when an accident caused paint on the bottom of the carrier to ignite. For several minutes until the fire burned itself out anxiety rose to an all-time high as the ship's bottom burned from stem to stern. Ordinarily, outbreak of a fire calls for the discharging over the side of inflammables and ordnance. This time, however, there was no water into which powder and shells could be dropped. Therefore, no order was given to do anything but search for hot-dogs and marshmallows and the carrier that would become the most decorated ship during World War Two "distinguished" herself by burning barnacles off her bottom in record time. It has been said by many that *Enterprise* was the one ship during the war that had a soul, and the incident just related is only one of many that seems to support that view.

Another incident that would seem to support the opinion that *Enterprise* had a soul was the timeliness of her recent wounds which put her in Pearl Harbor at the right moment. While in Pearl all four 1.1-inch "Chicago Piano" antiaircraft gun mounts were removed and in their place was installed the new 40mm quads. This weapon is generally recognized as being the most effective intermediate range antiaircraft gun of the war. On 16 October when the Big E left Pearl to return to the Solomons, among capital ships only she and her latest consort, newly arrived battleship *South Dakota,* possessed the dependable rapid fire 40mm guns. These guns would add a whole new dimension of excitement for Japanese aviators who would fly within six miles[1] of the two ships during the Battle of Santa Cruz.

Completion of repairs on *Enterprise* was not a minute too soon. Things were happening now in a hurry. Admiral Robert L. Ghormley, Commander South Pacific Force and Area was replaced on 18 October by an old friend of *Enterprise,* Admiral Bill Halsey. Halsey's first challenge was to meet the now forming, second major attempt by the enemy to recapture Guadalcanal. This time the Japanese would bring an even more powerful carrier force than had appeared on 24 August. Many biographers have written about Halsey's apprehension from 18 October until 24 October when his old flagship, *Enterprise,* appeared on the horizon and his spirits soared. Even though he realized he would still be outnumbered four or five enemy carriers to his two and outnumbered in battleships four to two, he believed he possessed the wherewithal to defend the tenuous hold on Guadalcanal. And he believed *Enterprise* would meet one more challenge for him. She would.

On 26 October *Enterprise* scout planes spotted the oncoming Japanese armada and the battle named for the nearby Santa Cruz Islands was on. Two *Enterprise* SBD scout bombers discovered the

---

[1]The range of the 1.1 "Chicago Piano" was approximately four miles. Five-inch guns had a range of 10 miles and the 20mm "close in" guns were effective up to 2½ miles.

Number three gun gallery. Note large bomb-entry hole.

USN

View of the extensive damage inside the carrier from the first two Eastern Solomons bombs. NA

A fire blackened 5-inch gun sits silently in the demolished starboard gun gallery. NA

enemy lightcarrier *Zuiho* and promptly placed two bombs on the aft portion of her flight deck. *Zuiho* would live to fight *Enterprise* again at a later time, but her role in this battle was terminated early. Air groups from both sides flew toward each other and both struck hard. *Hornet* would die before this day would end but her last hours in the service of her country were well spent. Her planes shattered *Shokaku's* flight deck and she accounted for her fair share of downed enemy planes.

In addition to those of *Shokaku* and *Zuiho*, planes from *Zuikaku* and *Junyo* flew against *Hornet* and *Enterprise*. At day's end the tactical victory had gone to Japan because *Hornet* had been sunk, but again strategic victory had gone to the United States. *Shokaku* and *Zuiho* were returning to safer water in search of new flight decks and undamaged *Zuikaku* and *Junyo* were returning west in search of new aircrews. Henderson Field was still in business, *Enterprise* was still afloat and daytime control of the water and air around Guadalcanal still belonged to America. The second great Japanese invasion force to fall upon Guadalcanal had been stopped and the fourth of the six major fleet-carrier battles was over.

Strategically successful as it was, tactically 26 October 1942 was a draw for *Enterprise*. Her scout planes had damaged *Zuiho*, but did no damage to any other enemy carriers. And again she suffered wounds. This time the carrier was hit by two bombs and although her damage was not as serious as the Eastern Solomon's affair she nonetheless lost 44 men and 75 were wounded. The first bomb traveled through the forward portion of the flight deck, the forecastle and then exited through the side of the ship. The second bomb, which caused the majority of the casualties, struck immediately behind the forward elevator and broke in two at the hangar deck with half continuing deep into the carrier. Two near misses severely damaged the hull and machinery.

The bright spots for the carrier in the Santa Cruz battle centered on defense. During this battle *Enterprise* encountered some 80 enemy planes in four separate dive bombing and torpedo attacks, one of the heaviest concentrations encountered by any ship during the war. In the air the Combat Air Patrol did outstanding work, especially against attacking torpedo planes. One pilot, Lt. Stanley Vejtasa, was credited with shooting down seven enemy planes in

The often produced classic picture of Enterprise *under attack during the battle of Santa Cruz 26 October 1942. Two enemy dive bombers are above the carrier and a bomb has just missed astern. Battleship* South Dakota *blazes away in the background.* NA

this fray and leading his squadron in the destruction of two others. On the water the Big E under the direction of new captain Osborne B. Hardison cut, turned, raced and reversed herself in a maddening pattern. Possessing a turning radius half that of the *Saratoga* and late *Lexington, Enterprise* combed nine torpedo wakes successfully and thereby escaped the weapons that rendered the major damage to the four American fleet-carriers lost in 1942. And in the gun galleries the 40mm was successfully introduced to the enemy. According to several men aboard *Enterprise* that day, enemy planes at times were falling on each other as they spiraled down in flames. Although the major credits for antiaircraft defense on 26 October must go to the sharp-shooting battleship *South Dakota* which was credited with 26 kills, *Enterprise* gunners had the satisfaction of watching the last several enemy dive bombers drop their bombs at a more respectful distance than had been the practice of earlier attackers.

With the battle over, *Enterprise,* with many *Hornet* planes also on board, sailed to the south to be out of the path of enemy surface ships but still close enough to Guadalcanal to meet defense needs there. This time there would be no time to return to Pearl for repairs. Of the six American fleet carriers to fight in the Pacific since the beginning of the war, *Enterprise* was the only operational carrier remaining. Four were gone forever and *Saratoga* would not be back for another two months. It was just as one crewman wrote on one of the carrier's bulkheads, *"Enterprise* against Japan." And it was this moment in history that inspired Eugene Burn's *Then There Was One,* referring to the several critical weeks when *Enterprise* was the only American carrier left to fight and hold the line. The book's title was borrowed from a quotation by Admiral Kincaid who alluded to the Pacific situation in November 1942 by saying "then there was one patched-up carrier."

Although *Enterprise* was not 100 percent—she could not operate her forward elevator and other Santa Cruz wounds were still open—she could still run at nearly top speed, operate all guns and launch her planes, although not as fast as usual. Therefore, she would move no further from Guadalcanal than Noumea for her repairs and she would stand ready to return to her station upon the first sign of trouble. It was expected that the Japanese would return in full force for a third time to settle the Guadalcanal issue and only three weeks later the sons of the Rising Sun were on their way southeast again.

NAVAL BATTLE OF GUADALCANAL

The four-day Naval Battle of Guadacanal (12-15 November 1942) was the final, all-out attempt by the Japanese to reinforce their garrison on the contested island. For slightly over three months Japanese forces on the island had attempted to retake Henderson Field and had failed, and on two occasions the Japanese carrier fleet had attempted

Near miss.   NA

to sweep the U.S. Navy from the southeastern Solomon's area. For their third major try at the two objectives just stated the Japanese packed 13,000 troops into eleven transports and sent two battleships along with cruisers and destroyers to support the thrust. But this time there would be no carriers. *Shokaku, Zuikaku* and *Zuiho* were either damaged or without sufficient aircrews. *Junyo* and *Hiyo* were at sea north of the battle site but were not committed to action in this climatic sea battle. Although a full explanation is not known why these last two enemy carriers did not support this operation, significant factors considered by the Japanese could have been that Henderson Field was "still a going concern" and an American carrier (*Enterprise*) was "snorting back and forth southward of Guadalcanal. (Mor. Vol. 5, pg. 286)

Upon learning the Japanese were gathering forces for their strongest push against Guadalcanal and due to the threat this posed not only to Henderson but also to American transports scheduled to arrive on 12 November, Admiral Halsey quickly ordered the Big E to return to attack position. The carrier sailed from Noumea on 11 November with planes and guns ready for action. A large contingent of crewmembers from the repair ship *Vestal* aboard worked furiously to repair the Santa Cruz battle damage. Still, watertight integrity was not fully restored and the forward elevator would not function.

Due to elevator problems, which slowed recovery and launching, a squadron of TBF Avengers were flown from *Enterprise* to Henderson Field. These Avengers and several *Enterprise* SBD Dauntlesses spent the 13th through the 15th flying into battle from both the carrier and the airstrip on an improvised shuttle system. But before *Enterprise* planes would see action the decisive battle began.

Under the relative safety of darkness on the night of November 12 a Japanese bombardment force entered Ironbottom Sound. This impressive force included cruisers, destroyers and battleship *Hiei* and the mission of these ships was to destroy Henderson Field or at least greatly disrupt air operations for the following day. However, a smaller force of American cruisers and destroyers met the enemy head on and turned away the Japanese from their main objective, the bombardment. The American success was costly. Six ships and two admirals (Daniel J. Callaghan and Norman Scott) were lost in the action. The Japanese lost two destroyers and the big battleship *Hiei* was severely wounded.

At sunrise on the 13th as *Hiei* was limping away from the battle area she was spotted by *Enterprise* airmen. In the early morning hours *Enterprise* and Marine Avengers flying from Henderson and SBDs flying from the carrier plastered *Hiei* until she went under just before dusk. The sailors who fought with Callaghan and Scott had prepared *Hiei* for death by

shooting her topsides full of holes during the night battle and *Enterprise* and Marine pilots finished the job. It was a good feeling for *Enterprise* airmen to see *Hiei* sinking into Ironbottom Sound. They knew *Hiei* was a threat to Guadalcanal and they would have been even more pleased had they known she was one of the two battleships accompanying the Pearl Habor attack. *Arizona* was partially avenged.

The failure of the Japanese bombardment force delayed the sailing of their transports on the 13th and another force, this one featuring the other battleship veteran of the Pearl Harbor raid—*Kirishima*, spent much of that night (13th) bombarding the Henderson airstrip and surrounding Marine entrenchments. Having been unopposed at sea during the night of the 13th the Japanese sent their eleven transports and escorting destroyers southeast early on the morning of the 14th. All day *Enterprise* Avengers from Henderson, SBDs from the carrier and Marine and Army pilots bombed and strafed the slow-moving transports. Before *Enterprise* SBDs attacked the transports they first searched for enemy carriers, found none and turned their attention to the heavy cruiser *Kinugasa*, which they sank. Then undivided attention was given to the transports.

Not enough can be said for the performance of ground crews at Henderson and aboard the carrier as they quickly prepared planes for return to "the "Slot," the sea path down the Solomons from Rabaul and other north Solomon Japanese bases to Guadalcanal. By dusk seven of the transports were sunk or sinking. The other four pushed on after dark and beached themselves on the Japanese held beaches of northeastern Guadalcanal. During the night of the 14th the same bombardment force that had appeared the previous evening returned to shoot up Henderson and help defend the four remaining transports. On this evening, however, two escorts of *Enterprise*—battleships *South Dakota* and *Washington*—were detached from America's lone Pacific carrier and sent forward to greet the enemy that 24 hours earlier had been unopposed. The ensuing fight was as desperate as the encounter two nights earlier and the result was much the same. The United States again lost more ships (all destroyers) but *Washington* caught *Kirishima* concentrating on *South Dakota* and shot her up so badly she had to be scuttled. In less than 48 hours the Japanese had lost their first two battleships of the war and had lost their last major bid to recapture the island.

With the sinking of *Kirishima* and the departure of the other enemy warships in the early morning hours of the 15th it was apparent the Japanese cause in the southern Solomon's was all but lost. And there would be another devastating blow to the enemy effort as *Enterprise* and Marine planes arrived over the beached transports and proceeded to blow them, many of their passengers, ammunition

An SBD is jarred off Enterprise's *flight deck by a bomb explosion during the Santa Cruz fight.* NA

Pictorial evidence of the many statements by Enterprise *crewmen that Japanese planes were practically falling on each other during the Battle of Santa Cruz. This battle was the introduction of the 40mm gun into combat.* NA

and supplies into oblivion. The carnage was horrendous and at the end of the day (15th) the Japanese could count only 2,000 of the original 13,000 troops aboard the transports on Guadalcanal, but without adequate food and supplies they were in no position to significantly influence the quest for the island.

The contest for Guadalcanal lasted another two and a half months. The enemy conceded control of the air above Guadalcanal to the United States and did not challenge American naval units in the area with either carriers or battleships after the middle of November. On 9 February 1943 the island was secured after the remaining 12,000 enemy troops were secretly withdrawn. The enemy left the island much in the manner in which he came—at night—so as to escape American planes. Although men on both sides continued to die on Guadalcanal until early Feburary 1943 and the two navies engaged in one further night surface battle (Tassafaronga, 30 November 1942), the Japanese did not again attempt a major effort to reinforce the island.

Many commentators have noted the fact that the United States Navy was willing to use its total strength in the decisive Santa Cruz and 12-15 November Guadalcanal naval battles. At Santa Cruz the U.S. Navy committed the only two carriers they had and during the Naval Battle for Guadalcanal used their only carrier (Enterprise) and only two modern battleships then operational. To the contrary Japan could have added ten battleships to the two utilized during the November battle and could have ordered in two to five carriers (in various degrees of readiness) instead of none. The student of Japanese military history must wonder why the super-battleships Yamato and Musashi were never committed to the fight in the Solomons. In 1942 these two ships could have made a real impact. When they were finally pointed to the scene of battle in 1944 it was too late and they were both lost for nothing.

Indeed next to Enterprise, the battleships Washington and South Dakota may have been the most important ships in the Solomons in making the difference between victory and defeat...a strong statement in view of the sacrifices and efforts of the many gallant American cruisers and destroyers that fought there. Other strong statements appearing from time to time in various histories of the Pacific War say that the United States actually won the war with Japan with the victory at Guadalcanal, and that the United States won the war with the ships it had in service at the beginning of the war. These last two statements are too absolute for this writer, but there is little argument that the war in the Pacific was about to acquire a new character as

The death of Hornet *(CV-8), stepsister to* Enterprise, *26 October 1942. Like* Lexington, Yorktown *and* Wasp *she "died hard." Even repeated attempts by her own escort failed to sink her. Japanese surface units finally administered the coup de grace.* NA

Funeral services aboard Enterprise *for the 44 crewmembers killed during the Battle of Santa Cruz.*   NA

the United States moved to an unrelenting offensive, and there is no argument that the pre-war ships of the U.S. Navy certainly proved their mettle in the dark, challenging days of 1942. If it cannot be said that they won the war, it must be said that they held the line against superior odds until their younger friends could join with them to push the remnants of the Imperial Japanese Navy back to the Inland Sea.

Between 15 November and 9 February *Enterprise* engaged in only one action remembered by name, the Battle of Rennell Island (29-30 Janaury 1943). Her role in this battle was defense of the heavy cruiser USS *Chicago*. *Chicago* had been struck by torpedoes from land-based enemy planes on the night of 29 January and *Enterprise* was ordered to cover her as she was towed toward safety. On the 30th a dozen enemy planes heading for *Chicago* changed course to strike *Enterprise,* but upon seeing the carrier's fighters in position to intercept, changed course again and placed four more tor-

pedoes into the the immobile American cruiser. *Enterprise* fighters and antiaircraft fire downed nearly all the attacking planes but that was small consolation for the ensuing loss of *Chicago.*

Despite the keen disappointment in not having been able to save *Chicago*, the six-month period of incessant fighting in the southern Solomon Islands must rank as the highlight of *Enterprise's* combat career. If the Big E had been lost at anytime between the day of the landings on 7 August '42 until the latter stages of the campaign the history of the Pacific War would have been different. The United States would not have lost the war but the price in lives and time would have been greatly expanded. Although *Enterprise's* role at Midway was critically significant, her performance day after day in the Solomons plus her major contributions during the three major enemy attempts to reinforce their Guadalcanal garrison garnered for her a unique and special place in American history.

An SBD flies over Enterprise *(foreground)* and Saratoga *as the two carriers patrol off Guadalcanal in late December 1942. By the date of this photograph* Enterprise *would never again have to fight or hold the line alone as she did in the November Naval Battle of Guadalcanal. The new Essex class carriers were about to join the fleet.* NA

CHAPTER SIX
1943: Year of Transition

World War Two in the Pacific was essentially two wars, particularly when viewed from the naval perspective. From December 1941 to December 1942 the United States and Japan met in four major fleet carrier battles, fought numerous surface actions, constantly challenged each other, and fought mostly with the men and ships that were on hand before 7 December 1941. During the year 1943 there were no fleet carrier battles, only a small number of surface actions, and the men and ships that had survived the intense fighting of 1942 were being replaced and supplemented by new men and new ships in numbers that surpassed the military might available at the beginning of the war. The year 1943, then, was a year of preparation and a year of transition. A war fought by regulars would now be fought to great extent by reserves and new recruits; a war fought with some World War One vintage combat ships would henceforth be fought with considerable new construction (mostly on the American side); and a war that had seen the United States basically on the defensive would now change character as the latter months of 1943 would witness the rapid thrust of a relentless, uninterrupted, several-pronged offensive that would carry American forces across the water and islands of the Pacific to the shores of Japan.

Enterprise suffered no damage in 1943 from the enemy. She did suffer accidents aboard and there would be losses to aircrews during training flights, but for the most part life aboard the carrier reflected the relative hiatus of the entire conflict in the Pacific for this year. After the Rennell Island scrap in January 1943, the Big E spent her time patrolling back and forth between Espiritu Santo and the southern Solomons. Guadalcanal was secured in February 1943 but the push would continue up the Solomons and *Enterprise* was needed to provide air cover for the movement of troop transports and supply ships. The period from January to May 1943 when *Enterprise* left the combat zone was uneventful because *Enterprise*, *Saratoga*, two escort-carriers and Henderson Field provided the United States with air superiority in the southern Solomon's, and because the Japanese carrier fleet was in great need of overhaul and new flight crews. They, like *Enterprise*, had been constantly at sea, giving and receiving blows and there now had to be a period of maintenance for the carriers and training for new air groups. In May word came to *Enterprise* ordering departure to Bremerton for her long overdue overhaul and she sailed to the mainland via Pearl.

Upon arrival at Pearl there was a delay of nearly two months before proceeding on to Bremerton as the ship was ordered to participate in training exercises for newly formed air groups. Onerous as this was to a crew anxious to return to the mainland of the United States (most of the crew had not been on the mainland in two years and the carrier had been away nearly four years), there was one event while at Pearl that definitely soothed the pervasive attitude of impatience. On 27 May 1943 men of the *Enterprise* dressed in whites and stood in formation to receive aboard Fleet Admiral Chester Nimitz. Admiral Nimitz awarded numerous decorations to *Enterprise* crewmembers and to men from other ships, but the highlight was his presentation to *Enterprise* on behalf of President Roosevelt the first ever Presidential Unit Citation awarded to an aircraft carrier. The Citation read:

> For consistently outstanding performance and distinguished achievement during repeated action against enemy Japanese forces in the Pacific war area, December 7, 1941, to November 15, 1942. Participating in nearly every major carrier engagement in the first year of the war, the Enterprise and her air group, exclusive of far-flung destruction of hostile shore installations throughout the battle area, did sink or damage on her own a total of 35 Japanese vessels and shoot down a total of 185 Japanese aircraft. Her aggressive spirit and superb combat efficiency are fitting tribute to the officers and men who so gallantly established her as an ahead bulwark in defense of the American nation.

Gilbert and Marshall Islands Raid	Feb. 1, 1942
Wake Island Raid	Feb. 25, 1942
Marcus Island Raid	March 4, 1942
Battle of Midway	June 4-6, 1942
Occupation of Guadalcanal	August 7-9, 1942
Battle of Stewart Islands (Eastern Solomons)	August 24, 1942
Battle of Santa Cruz Islands	Oct. 26, 1942
Battle of Solomon Islands (Naval Battle of Guadalcanal)	Nov. 14-15, 1942

Pearl Harbor was not mentioned in May 1943. Neither was the Halsey-Doolittle raid on Tokyo listed because "Shangri La" had not yet been announced.

Even some post-war corrections have failed to credit *Enterprise* with the famous April 18, 1942 attack, but the event was recorded on the carrier's hangar-deck bulkhead painting of the Citation.

The setting for this most significant award and recognition was quite appropriate. The day was sunny and the general atmosphere was positive as all knew the specter of possible defeat and loss of Hawaii had passed and that the future should bring success. However, a quick glance over the shoulder reminded all that the future would be perilous. The harbor area behind *Enterprise* on that 27th day of May was still not free from the wreckage of the infamous enemy raid nearly 18 months previous. *Oklahoma* still lay capsized and the shattered *Arizona* was still visible (her above-water superstructure was not removed until 1956). While these sights reminded one of future danger they also inspired resolve to complete the process of vengeance now half-accomplished.

After what seemed to be an interminable stay at Pearl, *Enterprise* was finally on her way to the mainland in mid-July. Crossing the Pacific from Pearl to Bremerton, Washington, was not as hazardous a voyage as those in or near combat zones and for the first time in longer than most could remember the word "leisure" re-entered vocabularies and its practice found expression. From the beginning of the war until after the battle of Midway, leisure and relaxation were not possible even if ordered by the Fleet Admiral himself. Especially during the first six months of the war tension was so high that mentally the crew would have been at battle stations if *Enterprise* had been tied up at the foot of Canal Street in New Orleans on the Mississippi River. But from the middle of 1942 until the beginning of the kamikaze attacks in late October 1944 there would

be occasions when some of the pursuits of a more normal time could be enjoyed.

Popular diversions aboard ship included field days, boxing, USO shows, movies, basketball and pollywog initiations. The nearly three-football-field-long flight deck was quite suitable for field days (track meets) and the enclosed hangar deck was adequate for basketball, boxing, movies and USO shows. Teams representing various ships would come aboard for the athletic competition and what was lacking in athletic skill at least passed for good entertainment. Comments from logs of the *Enterprise* detailed these events with as much enthusiasm as recording battle chronology. In one place a commentator wrote that a just completed boxing match was "three rounds of furious milling." Entertainment by professional performers was always well received with some of the top stars of the day appearing on *Enterprise*'s stage —a partially raised elevator. Dennis Day, Joe E. Brown and Tommy Riggs were among favorites to visit the carrier.

Movies were always welcome. All former crewmen seem to remember that *Sergeant York* was shown on the evening of 6 December 1941, but no one seems to remember the name of the movie that was about to be shown on 12 April 1943 when a bomb being used as a seat exploded and killed 16 men and wounded three dozen others.

One form of entertainment that is not remembered with a smile or a glow by *Enterprise* veterans (or veterans from any ship for that matter) was the initiation of "pollywogs"—new crewmembers who had not crossed the equator—to "shellbacks." These "Neptune Parties," which included officers as well as enlisted men, can only be likened to college fraternity hazings. And though it would be grand to report that

Enterprise off Espiritu Santo 13 April 1943.

USN

-56-

Fleet Admiral Chester Nimitz awards decorations to officers and men on the Big E's flight deck. In a similar cere-mony the Presidential Unit Citation was presented to Enterprise, *the first ever awarded to a carrier.*   NA

all interpersonal relations aboard *Enterprise* were close, cordial and patriotic above all else, truth will not allow such. Often bad feelings between two or more men began with the indignities inherent in the pollywog initiation. Other times men just simply did not interrelate well and, of course, there were times when leaders did not fully understand leadership. Forty years after the war some *Enterprise* veterans admit they would greet some of their old nemeses with a rotten tomato instead of a hand-shake, but such problems were the exception and not the rule. Otherwise, *Enterprise* or no other ship would have been equal to the demands of the era.

Just as the character of the war was changing in 1943, so was *Enterprise* about to reflect some of the changes during her overhaul period at the Puget Sound Navy Yard. From 20 July until late October *Enterprise* would sit in dry dock and receive treat-ment for 1942 battle damage, overhaul of essential machinery, electrical and communications

systems, and attention would be given to her metal skin from top to bottom. Naturally, these things would be done for any ship during an overhaul period in the yard. But the other attentions given to *Enterprise* reflected anticipation of the type of war to be fought in 1944 and 1945. First, provisions were made for more officers and enlisted men. Space, already at a premium, would now be even less available as more of everything from ammuni-tion to food would require accommodation.

Whereas the major allocations of space to serve the crew centered on food, bunks, lockers and air conditioning of some areas of the ship, other demands for a place on the already crowded carrier were in the interests of safety. New damage control equipment including sprinkler systems and independently operated fire mains were installed. It was expected that the new damage control system would be needed. It was.

It was also known in the summer of 1943 that the

A boxing match on Enterprise *in the Spring of 1943.* NA

An SBD pilot nears the tape to win the 220-yard dash during a field day aboard Enterprise. USN

Neptune party on Enterprise. *To some, these hazings were worse than attacks by the Japanese.* NA

anticipated movement of American carriers into enemy territory for sustained periods would require a stronger antiaircraft defense system. The 20mm guns would continue to be operated only by sight, but the 40mm and new, more powerful 5-inch rifles would be able to fire at unseen targets via newly installed radar controlled gunfire directors. No additional 5-inch guns were added to the carrier (still eight guns, two each near the four corners of the deck) but 14 additional 20mm guns were bolted down to bring the ship's total to 50, and 22 new additional 40mm barrels with supporting structures and power systems were installed. At this point in time *Enterprise* possessed 40 of the 40 mm guns in six quadruple groupings and eight dual groups. When the Big E left Bremerton in September 1945 only days after the war's end she was armed with 56 40mm guns—testimony to the need of knocking down kamikazes before they could reach the carrier.

For both safety against torpedoes and extra storage for fuel oil a large blister was welded to the sides of the carrier above and below the waterline. The carrier was growing in total displacement weight, length and width. Originally 19,800 tons, 809 feel long and 109 feet wide, *Enterprise* now registered an unloaded weight of over 21,000 tons, was 827 feet long and 114 feet wide. Finally, there was new metal along the front of the bridge and near the top front of the island. Requirements for more space dictated construction immediately below the tripod foremast and the bridge appearance changed from the previously squared contours to a rounded look much like the appearance of the late *Hornet's* bridge.

The transition, repair and modernization of the ship complete, *Enterprise* left the state of Washington and arrived at Pearl Harbor on 6 November. On board at the time of her arrival back at Pearl was a ship's company made up of nearly 40 percent new men, newer versions of the respected and battle proven SBD Dauntless, new and more efficient TBF Avengers and an altogether new fighter plane, the F6F Hellcat. The older F4F Wildcat would continue to contribute to the successful prosecution of the war and would remain in various combat theaters until the Japanese surrender. Flying mostly from escort carriers she played an important role and ended her days with a favorable 7 to 1 kill ratio over the enemy.

Despite the contributions of the F4F Wildcat and her longevity, mention of her name brings immediate scowls to the faces and a whole new vocabulary to the tongues of some former pilots who flew both the Wildcat and Hellcat. The best fighter plane available to the Navy in 1941, the Wildcat was nonetheless a medieval war chariot compared to the new Hellcat. Faster (386 mph to 318), more powerful (2,000 hp to 1,200), longer ranged (1,530 miles with drop tanks vs. 770 miles), and capable of carrying heavier ordnance (2,000 lbs. to 200) the Hellcat was a more formidable opponent for the Japanese Zero. Chief among the Hellcat pilots' appreciation, however, was the additional supply of ammunition for the six .50-caliber machine guns (400 rounds per gun to 200) and the considerable flying amenities within the cockpit such as switches in place of levers and electrically charged guns instead of manually operated guns. Being easier to fly and having more conveniences the Hellcat enabled its pilot to concentrate more fully on combat techniques. Thus, to a much greater degree he could dictate the tactics of air battle as

no American WW Two fighter could turn with or totally outmaneuver the Zero. From the time of her introduction into combat in mid-1943 until the close of the war in August 1945 the Hellcat would account for more enemy planes (5156) than any other Navy fighter and her kill ratio of 19 to 1 was also tops.

While on the subject of transition in main line combat planes, comment must be offered on a plane that proved her worth, had tremendous credentials for her time, a high kill ratio (11 to 1), but was still the most under-used Navy fighter of the war...the F4U Corsair. The rugged gull-winged Corsair had a top speed of 415 mph, the longest range of any Navy fighter (1,560 + with drop tanks) and could carry ordnance weights up to 3,000 pounds, more than some bombers could carry. But, the relatively far aft location of the cockpit hindered pilot's vision of flight decks and her landing speed was thought to be too high for carrier decks and therefore the fighter was originally assigned only to Marine units to be flown from land bases even though the British were using them on carriers. Available to the Navy before the Hellcat, the Corsair could have made her mark on naval

Head-on view of Enterprise *at Puget Sound 21 October 1943.*   NA

Enterprise *at the Puget Sound Navy Yard 19 October 1943 at the time of the inclining experiment.*
Note new 40mm installations and new bridge. USN

aviation before she did and would have been especially welcome aboard *Enterprise* during the Solomon Island campaign. As it was the Corsair appeared on the deck of *Enterprise* for the first time in the spring of 1943 on a training mission and never did operate in large numbers from the Big E. Most Corsairs aboard *Enterprise* in 1944 and 1945 operated primarily in night fighter roles and in this role her range and ability to carry radar made her particularly effective.

Another sign of transition in November 1943 to greet *Enterprise* at Pearl was the sight of some of the new Essex-class carriers and the cruiser-hulled light carriers (CVL's) that could operate at fleet speed. During 1943 seven new Essex-class carriers joined the fleet: *Essex* CV-9 (commissioned 31 December 1942), the second *Lexington* CV-16, the second *Yorktown* CV-10, *Bunker Hill* CV-17, *Intrepid* CV-11, the second *Wasp* CV-18 and the second *Hornet* CV-12. These seven were to become the most notable of the superb Essex-class carriers during World War Two. Class leader *Essex* received 13 battle stars, *Lexington*, *Yorktown* and *Bunker Hill* received 11, *Wasp* 8, *Hornet* 7, and *Intrepid* 5. These ships, except badly wounded *Bunker Hill*, would join with other carriers of the class to enter the fleet

in 1944 and 1945 (minus also badly damaged *Franklin* CV-13) to serve the United States well beyond the end of World War Two. At the time of this writing (1982) only *Lexington* (now AVT-16) is still in operation, but few military allocations have returned such longevity and quality of service as that of the Essex-class fleet-carriers.

All nine light carriers (11,000 tons and 622 feet long) were commissioned in 1943 and were known by the name of class leader *Independence* (CVL-22). *Belleau Wood* CVL-24, *Monterey* CVL-26, and *Cowpens* CVL-25 each were awarded 11 battle stars while *Cabot* CVL-28 and *Langley* CVL-27 received 9, *San Jacinto* CVL-30 won 7 and *Bataan* CVL-29 recorded 5. *Princeton* CVL-23 would become the only member of the class to be lost in combat (Battle of Leyte Gulf, 24 October 1944), and *Independence*, like *Enterprise*, would spend much of 1944 and 1945 as a night operations carrier. Addition of the Essex-class carriers and the nine light carriers to *Enterprise*, *Saratoga* and several dozen escort carriers provided the wherewithal for American advancement across the Pacific. *Enterprise* would now have to share news accounts with the newer carriers, but it was comforting in 1944-45 to be one of many instead of one of few or the only

Chart of cross-section of Enterprise *showing original design.*   NA

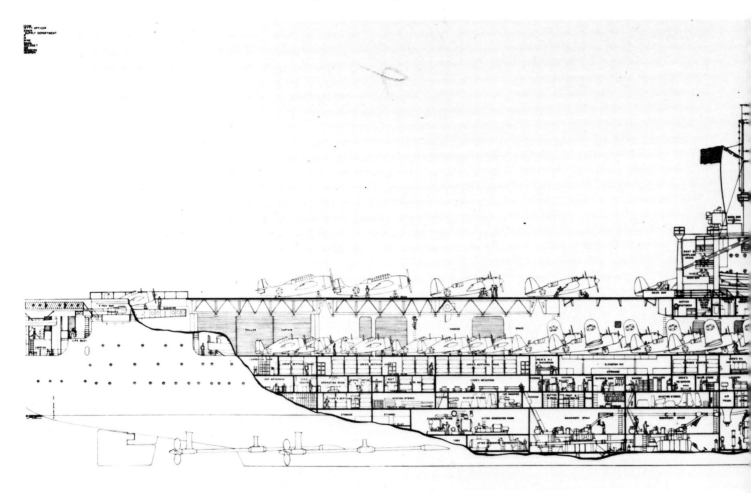

one. Her exploits in 1942's critical battles had already made her a recognized legend. Then, as now, her place in naval annals was secure.

Many stories abound concerning what the appearance of *Enterprise* meant to various sailors. The most famous story—Halsey's reaction when *Enterprise* arrived before the battle of Santa Cruz—has already been told, but another tale relates to the return of *Enterprise* in November 1943. One of the more notable admirals was surveying the new carriers, battleships and cruisers in the harbor but seemingly could not capture the positive, enthusiastic attitude he felt he should have. At that moment *Enterprise* came into view and the admiral picked up his cap and told an aide, "if *Enterprise* is ready to fight, so am I." Despite *Enterprise's* capacity to inspire admirals, her appearance to others often produced different sentiments. To some *Enterprise* was a floating prison that kept them from home, family, friends and safety. And to others the appearance of *Enterprise* meant that trouble was not far away; wherever she went there would be fighting. Finally, her appearance was a thing of beauty to the aforementioned Japanese sailor who thought she was a new Japanese carrier when *Enterprise* and *Hornet* were approaching his homeland for the April 1942 Tokyo raid. We can assume *Enterprise* became very

ugly very fast to the enemy sailor when her planes began attacking his patrol boat.

The days spent in Pearl were few because it was time for *Enterprise* and her new floating friends to return to work. The transition period of the war was over and now American forces were prepared to attack, neutralize and/or occupy enemy bases in the South Pacific, southwestern Pacific and central Pacific. Central Pacific enemy bases in the Marshalls and Gilberts had been raided from February 1942 when *Enterprise* and the first *Yorktown* paid a visit, up until the summer of 1943 when the second *Yorktown*, second *Lexington* and other new ships struck. This time, however, America was coming to stay.

For *Enterprise* the Gilbert Islands operation beginning on 19 November 1943 would be another first. Along with other carriers she would be part of the first central Pacific occupation. The target for *Enterprise* was Makin in the northern Gilberts and while pilots from the Big E were bombing, strafing and providing aerial observation for the operation commander, Marines were methodically clearing the major areas of resistance. Nearly 100 miles south other U.S. Marines were having a much tougher go at Tarawa; nonetheless, in less than a week, the major enemy bases in the Gilberts had changed ownership. Although primed and ready

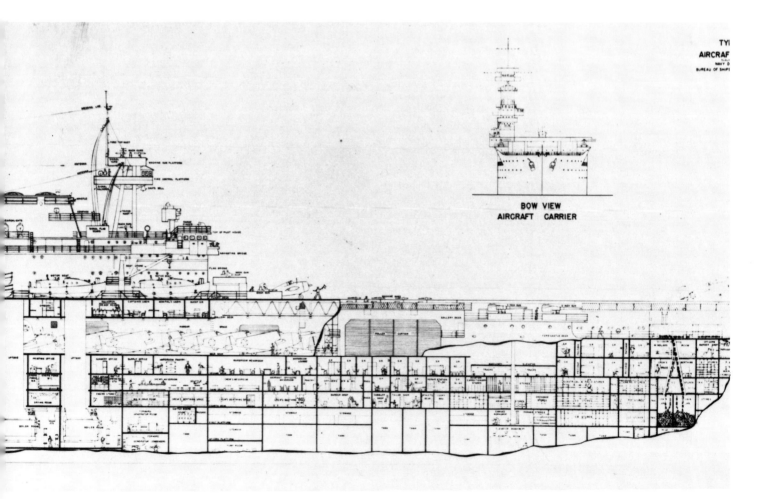

BOW VIEW
AIRCRAFT CARRIER

for a Japanese carrier-led counterattack, none developed. Japanese carriers were still training and their next sortie would be in defense of critical bases. The Gilberts and Marshalls were not on the critical list in late 1943.

Even though the Gilberts' occupation did not bring out the Japanese carriers, it did mark the occasion of a new enemy tactic—night air attack. On the evening of the 25th of November enemy torpedo planes began dropping parachute flares and then attacking. What happened on the following night (26th) is reminiscent of the World War One occurrence of the invention of a machinegun geared to fire through a propeller—a major armament breakthrough—only to see the opposition develop the same weapon within 24 hours. When the Japanese torpedo planes arrived after dark on the 26th, *Enterprise* had a "bat team" airborne to greet them. The idea of how to fight a night battle originated with Lt. Comdr. Bill Martin, Cmdr. Tom Hamilton (both would retire as admirals) and Lt. Cmdr. Butch O'Hare, the famous fighter pilot who had won the Medal of Honor for attacking alone a flight of nine Japanese planes and shooting down five while flying off the first *Lexington* in 1942. On the night of the 26th O'Hare was piloting one of two Hellcats that were led to the enemy planes by a radar-carrying Avenger. The idea was to have the Avenger lead the fighters to the enemy and then let the fighters sight the blue exhaust flame of the enemy plane and then shoot. This historic flight was the first night carrier-plane interception and it

was successful. Two enemy planes were shot down and more may have been lost as the confused and surprised Japanese planes began to shoot at each other. As with other successes during the war, however, the price of this victory was high. Whereas Commander Stafford in *THE BIG E* only suggests the rear gunner in the Avenger mistakenly shot down Butch O'Hare, R.W. Gregory who was listening in CIC to the pilots talking with one another during the battle is convinced that is what happened. Gregory and others heard O'Hare's voice, heard the gunfire and then heard only silence.

The action on the evening of 26 November presaged a future chapter in the life of *Enterprise*. In the not-too-distant future she would officially assume duties as a night carrier (first fleet-carrier so designated) to continue the tactics pioneered by her men.

No longer needed in the Gilberts, *Enterprise* sailed north to the Marshalls to assist in the strikes there. These strikes were preliminary to the occupation effort which would come the following month and *Enterprise* air groups joined in the bombing and strafing. In the late evening of 4 December the new *Lexington* was struck by aerial torpedo during a parachute-flare attack and Rear Admiral Charles Pownall, the second captain of *Enterprise* now in command of these strikes, withdrew his forces and ordered departure for Pearl. Less than two months later, however, *Enterprise* and friends would return, next time to stay.

The second Lexington *CV-16 at sea. The Essex-class carriers featured a pyramid island structure, deck edge elevator amidships, and 5-inch gun turrets fore and aft of the island.*   USN

CHAPTER SEVEN
The Marianas and Leyte Gulf: Fleet Carrier Battles Five and Six

It was well anticipated in both the United States and Japan that 1944 would be a decisive year for their respective navies and war fortunes. American forces now had not only the sea power to challenge the long-held Japanese defense plan, but also had developed a strategy to counter it. The Japanese plan evolved from the theory that a series of island bases would form an outer perimeter to (1) allow detection of the advancing Americans, (2) permit planes from the island bases to mutually support each other when one base was attacked, and (3) serve as a point of contact for major Japanese Fleet units to sail to from their protected anchorages in the inner perimeter. Not only would the Japanese major fleet units be in position from their advantageous interior lines, they would be able to meet American forces well away from the Japanese mainland and away from critically important sea routes serving Japan's importation of resources and distribution of war materiel and troops.

The Japanese defensive plan just mentioned did not succeed because (1) the American counter-strategy was to attack all bases in an island group at the same time—a tactic now possible due to the large and growing number of available aircraft carriers and (2) when battle was joined, Japanese airmen were not the equal of their American adversaries. Loss of their best aircrews in the battles of 1942, lack of fuel for training, and miscalculation of the length of the war resulting in fewer available pilots were some of the more salient reasons for the declining performances of Japanese airmen in 1944 and 1945. Had the Japanese been able to win air battles, the American counter-strategy would have been negated.

Even though their strategy would fail, the Japanese anxiously awaited meeting the U.S. Navy in fleet-strength decisive battle. The U.S. Navy was equally anxious and both sides would get their wish in 1944. But before the two final major sea battles of the war, there would first be some necessary preliminaries to set the stage. These began for the U.S. Navy and *Enterprise* just as 1943, the year of transition, became 1944, the year of decision.

With American naval power growing with the passing of each day and numerous new units now available, a new organizational structure was introduced in the form of task forces (TF's, Fast Carrier Forces) built around three or four fast carriers supported by new, fast battleships, cruisers and destroyers. This structure would exist through the remainder of the war and prove to be capable of meeting all challenges to it. During the final 20 months of the Pacific war these task forces would be at sea constantly and there would be no period of rest for the enemy.

Enterprise joined the new *Yorktown* and light carrier *Belleau Wood* for her first sortie under the new organization when Task Force 58 sailed in late January 1944 to strike the Marshall Islands. The main landings were on Kwajalein between 29 January and 3 February, but *Enterprise, Yorktown* and *Belleau Wood* were responsible for the destruction of other island bases (Taroa particularly) from which enemy pilots would attempt to help their fellows on Kwajalein. This battle would not be as furious in the air or on land as many to follow, but it was nonetheless an important and necessary victory.

The return trip from support of the Marshall's occupation was more interesting. In fact, it was a little too interesting for many. The task force was going to strike the inner perimeter "impregnable" Japanese air and naval base at Truk in the Caroline Islands. Despite considerable negative premonitions concerning such an assignment and still somewhat unsure of how strong her new muscles were, the force closed and attacked on 17 February. The initial fighter sweep was led by *Enterprise's* Lt. Commander William R. (Killer) Kane during the early morning strike. Results during the day were good, but the events after dark were excellent as *Enterprise* registered another naval aviation first; a night radar bombing attack. Bill Martin's 12 Avengers registered outstanding results for the night's work by sinking approximately 65,000 tons of shipping and thereby accounted for nearly one-third of the enemy tonnage lost to TF 58 planes during this first assault on Truk.

Detached from TF 58, *Enterprise* raided Jaluit Atoll on 20 February, replenished at Majuro and Espiritu Santo and then provided air cover for the occupation of Emirau Island 19-25 March. Rejoining TF 58 on 26 March *Enterprise* and other carriers spent the following two weeks striking Yap, Ulithi (a future anchorage), Woleai and Palau Islands (site of

A Japanese destroyer explodes from direct hits by Enterprise *SBDs during the strike on the Palau Islands 30 March 1944.*

NA

Peleliu—a vicious battle fought by Marines in September 1944 and historically remembered as "the killing ground.") On 22 April *Enterprise,* the second *Lexington*—with whom she would fight beside for most of 1944—and other carriers supported landings in the Hollandia area of New Guinea and on 29-30 April the force again hit Truk in a neutralization strike. The attack on Truk was the last of the preliminaries; it was now time for the main events.

BATTLE OF THE PHILIPPINE SEA

On the 6th of June 1944, D-Day in Europe, TF 58 sortied from the anchorage at Majuro toward the Mariana Islands. Over 500 American ships were committed to this operation which began on 11 June. Between 11 and 14 June *Enterprise* air groups attacked Saipan—site of the major landings on 15 June—Rota and Guam and then supported the landings on the 15th, 16th and 17th.

Whereas the Japanese Combined Fleet was not inclined to defend their outer perimeter bases in the Marshall's or Gilbert's, the Marianas battle was one in which there was no choice. American suc-

cess in occupying the Marianas would mean two things totally unacceptable to the Japanese: (1) shipping lanes between the southern Pacific resource areas and Japan would be cut by U.S. land-based planes, and (2) American Army Air Corps heavy bombers would be able to strike the Japanese homeland (indeed, the B-29 that carried the atom bomb to Hiroshima flew from Tinian in the Marianas). To meet the Marianas invasion Japan called forth her best for the duel. Converging on the Philippine Sea immediately west of the Marianas came her only three fleet carriers (old *Enterprise* antagonists *Shokaku* and *Zuikaku* and the new *Taiho*), six light carriers (*Zuiho, Ryuho, Junyo, Hiyo, Chitose* and *Chiyoda*) and other combat ships including the overprotected super-battleships *Yamato* and *Musashi.* The forthcoming battle was only an opportunity for the United States: for Japan the critical battle meant victory or sure defeat in the war.

Japanese hopes for victory were supported by their advantage of interior lines, support from land-based planes within flying distance of the Marianas, planes with longer range and a wind direction allowing them to maintain a course toward the bat-

Hellcats are moved into position aboard Enterprise, *February 1944.*

USN

-67-

tle area while American carriers would have to turn away from the fight to launch and recover. It was believed these advantages could offset the American advantage in carriers (seven fleet carriers including *Enterprise, Lexington, Essex, Wasp, Bunker Hill, Hornet* and *Yorktown* plus eight light carriers including *Princeton, San Jacinto, Belleau Wood, Bataan, Langley, Cowpens, Cabot* and *Monterey*). The 15 American carriers were carrying upwards of 950 planes to fly against approximately 450 Japanese carrier-borne planes and nearly 200 land-based aircraft.

The approach of the Japanese Fleet was well-known even as it began. Numerous U.S. submarine reports filtered into Admiral Spruance, who was in overall command of the operation, and to Admiral Marc Mitscher in command of the carriers of TF 58. Even though the submarine reports indicated the Japanese were on the way, the relatively short searching range of American planes did not allow a sighting of the Japanese Fleet before the 19th of June when the battle began. On the 19th American scout planes and radar picked up the incoming Japanese planes, fighters were vectored out to meet them and the "greatest carrier battle" of the war was on.

The Battle of the Philippine Sea, better remembered as the "Marianas Turkey Shoot" was strictly a defensive battle on the 19th as Japanese planes could reach the American force but the still unlocated Japanese force was too far away to be attacked. The "greatest carrier battle" is so called because of the great number of carriers and planes involved. It was not the greatest battle of the war for American war fortunes although it may be argued that it was for Japanese fortunes.

Before the opening of the battle there was a feeling of the drama about to unfold. This would be the first fleet-carrier battle in over a year and a half, the fifth of the war, and the first one to be fought in what could be called Japanese waters. Drama was rather quickly lost on the 19th, however, as it became apparent a rout was in the making. The day of the 19th can be likened unto a football game matching two teams apparently equal on paper. Great excitement attends the period before the game, but when one team takes a four-touchdown lead in the first quarter, drama is gone and the victory party begins.

For men aboard the *Enterprise,* the only American carrier present that had ever participated in a fleet battle, initial anticipation was that this battle

One of the few Japanese planes to penetrate the CAP during the Battle of the Philippine Sea falls astern of Enterprise *19 June 1944.*

NA

would be similar to the old Solomons' battles. It was not to be a carbon copy: of the 400-plus enemy planes that flew against the American Fleet only two or three dozen even sighted the American force and fewer actually attacked. Antiaircraft guns aboard *Enterprise* anticipated a very busy day, but it turned out quite easy. *Enterprise* did fire on several attacking planes and shared credit for downing the handful of attacking planes that came within range (see photo of one *Enterprise* victim).

It is difficult to provide a dramatic blow by blow description of the air battle because it was too one-sided to be dramatic. Seen by radar, scout planes and by their own contrails, the relatively inexperienced and, as the events of the day proved, undisciplined enemy pilots were little challenge to American fighters. Before the two-day battle was over the Japanese losses were 426 carrier planes, several dozen land-based planes on Guam (thanks in part to visitation by *Enterprise's* air groups) and three carriers—*Taiho* and *Shokaku* on the 19th to U.S. submarines *Albacore* and *Cavalla* respectively and *Hiyo* on the 20th to carrier planes, CVL *Belleau Wood* given credit for the sinking.

On the 19th *Enterprise* fighters joined fighters from other carriers in the carnage high above the Philippine Sea and collected their fair share of victims. Meanwhile SBDs, Avengers and Hellcats from *Enterprise* were striking nearby Guam. There, the *Enterprise* planes destroyed enemy aircraft on the ground and in the air, dropped bombs with delayed fuses into landing strips to hinder night take-offs and generally created havoc and destruction to repair shops, ammunition dumps, fuel storage and anything else militarily valuable.

On the 20th *Enterprise* perhaps made her most important contribution to the battle by finally locating for TF 58 the now retiring enemy fleet. The *Enterprise* report of the sighting came late in the afternoon and the resultant American air strike occurred just before sundown. *Enterprise* pilots attacked *Zuikaku*, *Chiyoda*, *Junyo*, *Ryuho* and *Hiyo*. Near misses were recorded and the few hits did not strike vital parts. *Hiyo* was sunk, however, and two oilers were lost by the enemy to the several air groups representing the American carriers.

The exciting story of events of 20 June 1944 was not so much the chasing and sinking of Japanese ships. Returning to their carriers in total darkness American planes were lost and nearly out of fuel. From the bridge of *Lexington* came the courageous decision of Admiral Marc Mitscher to disdain enemy submarines and to turn on all ships' lights to help planes find carrier decks. Although many returning planes still had to ditch for lack of fuel and most ended up landing on a carrier other than their own, pilots were saved by the dozens who most assuredly would have been lost without the assistance of Mitscher. *Enterprise* losses during this

sortie were amazingly low; only a half dozen planes were lost and no pilots. For the entire task force less than 100 aircrew members were lost.

Despite the lopsided victory American perceptions of the battle were not satisfactory. Belief was that the Japanese Fleet should have been pursued more vigorously. Although most historians agree that the battle was correctly fought by American commanders—defend Siapan landings first and strike enemy sea forces second—the desire to confront and destroy Japanese naval air power became an obsession that would overwhelm some naval commanders in the Battle of Leyte Gulf four months hence. At the conclusion of the war's fifth fleet-carrier battle, the U.S. Navy not only did not know that *Shokaku* and *Taiho* had been sunk, but also did not know that Japanese carrier-borne airpower was no longer a serious threat.

BATTLE OF LEYTE GULF

After the battle of 19-20 June, *Enterprise* continued to support the Marianas campaign through 5 July and then sailed for Pearl Harbor for overhaul and replenishment. During this stay in Pearl, *Enterprise* received a special paint job designed to help camouflage her identity and hopefully mislead enemy airmen and submarines regarding her speed and direction. Also, *Enterprise* received aboard a new bomber to replace the SBD Dauntless. The new bomber was the SB2C Curtiss Helldiver—well-liked by Commander (now retired Rear Admiral) Emmett Riera, leader of *Enterprise's* Bombing Twenty, but not well-liked by other pilots and particularly disliked by plane handlers.

Replenishment complete and paint dry, the Big E returned to the combat theater and participated with TF 38 in aerial assaults on the Volcano and Bonin Islands (31 August-2 September), Yap, Ulithi and the Palaus (6-8 September). On 7 October 1944 *Enterprise* sailed from waters west of the Palau Islands to join with other units of TF 38 to strike Okinawa, Formosa and the Philippines in preparation for General MacArthur's return to the Philippines. At this time things were going so well for the allied cause in the Pacific that other planned preliminary raids were deleted and the big thrust into the Philippines was moved up appreciably. Things were going so well, in fact, that *Enterprise* departed the Philippines on 20 October to return to Ulithi for replenishment, but on the 23rd word came that the Japanese Fleet was at sea again and headed for the site of the American invasion—Leyte Gulf. The sixth and last fleet-carrier battle of the war was imminent and *Enterprise* turned and raced back to engage.

Of the three separate actions comprising the Battle of Leyte Gulf on 24-25 October 1944, *Enterprise* was the only carrier to strike all three enemy

Generally accepted as the classic picture of Enterprise, *this photo was taken from the rear seat of a just departed SBD, July 1944.* NA

groups at each of the three action sites. Early on 24 October *Enterprise* and *Franklin* planes located the enemy Southern Force and attacked. Hits were made on a cruiser and on the battleships *Fuso* and *Yamashiro* but damage was insufficient to turn them back. It would have been better for these ships if they had turned back because that night they would run directly into an American force comprised in part of Pearl Harbor battleship victims *West Virginia, Tennessee, Pennsylvania, California* and *Maryland* (plus *Mississippi*) and would be annihilated in the battle of Surigao Strait.

Later on the afternoon of the 24th *Enterprise* air groups attacked the Center Force and during what would become known as the Battle of the Sibuyan Sea, *Enterprise* had the pleasure and distinction of participating meaningfully by placing several bombs and torpedoes into one of Japan's super-battleships, *Musashi.* The big battlewagon dipped beneath the surface before dark and by sundown the Center Force was retiring and apparently in retreat.

In the time that *Enterprise* air groups were attacking the Center Force, the third Japanese Force (Northern) was sighted. During the night of the 24th, ten fast carriers (*Enterprise, Lexington, Essex, Franklin, Intrepid* and CVL's *Independence, Belleau Wood, San Jacinto, Cabot* and *Langley*) roared north to meet the Northern Force and during the day of the 25th, the American air groups jumped *Zuikaku, Zuiho, Chiyoda* and *Chitose* and sank all four in the Battle off Cape Engano. *Enterprise* was particularly involved in the sinking of *Zuiho* and just as one of the more notable pictures of the mortally damaged *Musashi* was taken by an *Enterprise* plane after it had dropped its ordnance on the battleship, so also was a notable picture of the damaged *Zuiho* taken by an *Enterprise* airman just after he had launched a torpedo at the doomed carrier.

Despite the overwhelming victory off Cape Engano, the Japanese Northern Force was a decoy. The ruse almost worked. Still smarting from perceived unsatisfactory achievement in the June Marianas fight, the fast carrier force including *Enterprise* took the bait of the four enemy carriers and was well out of range when the Center Force reversed itself and suddenly appeared from San Bernadino Straits off Samar and headed toward the landing area in Leyte Gulf. With enemy heavy units coming down on the landing beaches and American battleships and carriers now far to the north, a situation was developing much akin to that immediately after the Savo Island debacle just after the initial assault on Guadalcanal in August 1942. But, whereas in the first five fleet battles American victory could be assigned to men flying from fast fleet carriers, victory in the Leyte Gulf battle of 24-25 October 1944 must be shared by fleet-carrier pilots with the outgunned destroyers and escort carriers that courageously defended transports and troops in the action off Samar.

Throughout the war in the Pacific at least two patterns developed in fleet-carrier confrontation. First was the concentrated time pattern. There were to be six major carrier battles. Four of these were fought in 1942 (Coral Sea, Midway, Eastern Solomons and Santa Cruz) all within a six-month period. The final two were fought in 1944 within a period of four months. The second pattern was that of Japanese premature withdrawal. In five of the six battles—the June Philippine Sea battle the only exception—the Japanese withdrew too soon. During the Battle of Leyte Gulf only one of the three Japanese sea forces withdrew too soon, but that one—Center Force off Samar—was the one that counted.

The Battle of Leyte Gulf was the last fleet-carrier battle of the war and it was also the last battle between surface units of any meaningful number. From October 1944 until the end of the war in August 1945 the Japanese Navy was impotent. The Japanese, however, did sink CVL *Princeton* during the Leyte battle—the last fast carrier of the five the United States would lose in the war. And on the 29th of October, only four days after the Leyte sea battle ended, men aboard *Enterprise* got their first look at the most efficient Japanese weapon of the war...the kamikaze. On the 29th *Enterprise* was attacked by a suicider, but missed. However, *Enterprise* gunners and others topside did see *Franklin* and *Belleau Wood* take serious hits in the same hour. Since the battles in the Solomon Islands in 1942, *Enterprise* had had it relatively easy; antiaircraft batteries had been relatively quiet and life aboard was considered nowhere near as dangerous as it had been two years previous. But the first kamikaze strike on 29 October changed all that. It was 1942 all over again.

Enterprise *departing Pearl Harbor 2 August 1944 with her new dazzle paint job.*　　　**NA**

A damaged Avenger returns to Enterprise *25 October 1944 during the Battle of Leyte Gulf.*　　USN

Japanese superbattleship Musashi *under attack by* Enterprise *planes 24 October 1944 in the Sibuyan Sea. Picture was taken from an* Enterprise *plane after its ordnance had been deposited into* Musashi. *The giant battleship sank later in the day.*　　NA

Japanese carrier Zuiho 25 October 1944. After four battles with Zuiho, planes from Enterprise and other carriers finally sank her on this date. This often-produced photo was taken from an Enterprise Avenger just after dropping a torpedo which hit Zuiho seconds after this picture was snapped. NA

One final banzai for the Emperor and a salute to the naval ensign before Zuikaku, last of the six enemy carriers to strike Pearl Harbor, rolls over and sinks 25 October 1944. USN

CHAPTER EIGHT
The Defensive Offensive: 1944-1945

The relentless offensive begun in late 1943 was continuing at a progressive rate, but the approach to the Japanese mainland and the threat of kamikazes added a special emphasis to defense. Therefore, the period from late October 1944 until the signing of the truce in August 1945 was in fact a defensive offensive.

With the introduction of kamikaze attacks in late October 1944, the attitude of *Enterprise* crewmembers changed radically. The previous inner feelings of optimism regarding a favorable conclusion of the war and its near termination was now overwhelmed by more pertinent fears for preserving life against the fearful new enemy weapon. Without question the kamikaze caused more concern than the unfavorable odds *Enterprise* had faced during the Solomon Islands days. In 1942 there was a quiet belief deep within that the enemy could be beaten in face to face confrontations and each American victory added support to that conviction. But in late 1944 there suddenly appeared in the form of the kamikaze attacks an element so unprecedented and unconventional that the psyche of the American sailor initially approached a state of anomie; a loss of norms, a loss of knowledge of one's place and purpose in war. In a sailor's language, the kamikaze attacks "weren't fair play," and as in any contest, failure to play by known and accepted rules often produces a disconcerted disposition within an opponent. In time anomie would dissipate and in its place would appear a determination to fight and survive that approached the ruthlessness of the kamikaze in expression. Even so, the "game" of war was over. Jokes, smiling faces and conversations of home diminished markedly and there would no longer be the half-serious bantering between ships' gunners and pilots to "let one (enemy plane) come on through so we'll have something to shoot at."

Daily routine also changed after October 1944 and became even more onerous than it had ever been. Men were accustomed to going to General Quarters just before sunrise, just before sundown and when engaging the enemy. In the past, usually five or six hours a day was all that would be required at GQ. Now, any time *Enterprise* was not riding at anchor in the relative safety of Pearl Harbor or Ulithi lagoon she would constantly be at GQ and

ready for the new threat that could be expected at any moment of the day or night and in numbers ranging from one to "many." When asked to recall the first thought coming to mind when thinking of those kamikaze days characterizing the last months of the war, the first reply from most former *Enterprise* men is "we never got any sleep." At least one crewmember believes he defied science in all that time by never getting more than three hours sleep a day. The second recollection of that era is the quality of food consumed while at battle stations. Eating good food from plates in mess halls became a rare event since the crew was so often at GQ. At battle stations canned rations were issued and occasionally to break the monotony special treats—like spaghetti served from buckets—were brought to the men. Not surprisingly, many *Enterprise* veterans have not since been able to wave a fork at a plate of spaghetti.

Enterprise was fortunate not to be at sea during the infamous typhoon of December 1944, but she did ride through two others. On the 8th and 9th of November 1944 the carrier traveled through the southern portion of one. Ordinarily a typhoon is not welcome, but since such a storm means no air operations for either antagonist, this one was almost welcome. Also, the interlude from battle meant a decent meal. Two long lines formed on the hangar deck and the pitching and rolling of the ship only slightly diminished appetites waxing anxious for the culinary delight at the front of the two lines. Suddenly, however, the tossing waves caused a crated engine to break loose. Fortunately, no one was injured but as the ship continued to pitch and roll the big, heavy engine slid ponderously across the deck scattering first one line of impatient and hungry sailors and then chasing men in the other line. This went on for several minutes and at first the famished men were more concerned about their daily bread and place in line than the engine-turned-billiard-ball, but as it continued to disrupt and disperse the lines, some finally attempted to stabilize the errant machinery. Best efforts did little as the engine continued to slam against bulkheads, only now it carried a dozen or so passengers. At long last the engine worked its way down the deck and fell into the number two elevator pit and the ship's crew, after working up an even greater appetite while running from and chasing after the engine, reformed their lines and awaited their long overdue repast.

After the momentous Battle of Leyte Gulf, *Enterprise* patrolled east of Samar and Leyte until the end of October, returned to Ulithi for supplies and then sailed back to the Philippines. On 11 November planes from *Enterprise* and other TF 38 carriers intercepted a Japanese troopship convoy attempting to reinforce the Philippine garrison. The rather short contest between the American planes and the enemy convoy was quite one-sided and when the planes departed six transports were sunk or sinking and two destroyers were down. On the 13th of November *Enterprise* planes were in the air again to strike airfields and shipping in the Manila region and in so doing hit the jackpot in finding and destroying hidden planes.

A return to Pearl Harbor on 6 December marked an end to one era for *Enterprise* and the beginning of another. When the big carrier sailed again on 24 December to return to the Philippines, she carried an air group specially trained for night-carrier operations. *Enterprise* would not be exempt from daytime activities, but her major mission now was to harass the enemy at night and help cover the period of time at the end of daylight and again just before sunrise. Her responsibilities would be both offensive and defensive—just like the day carriers—but her emphasis would be on the tactics that had been pioneered by Bill Martin, Tom

Hamilton, the late Butch O'Hare, radar operators and others within her. Martin's theory on night radar attacks dated from 1942; the practice of night interception dated from the first flight from *Enterprise* 26 November 1943, and the first successful, significant night radar attack dated from the *Enterprise* raid on Truk 17 February 1944. It was only appropriate that *Enterprise* now concentrated on the form of warfare developed on her decks. And it was appropriate that Bill Martin would be commander of Night Air Group Ninety and that former captain Mat Gardner, now Admiral Gardner, would be in command of the special night operations carriers.

The light carrier *Independence* was the first fast carrier to assume the primary responsibility of a night carrier (summer 1944) and *Enterprise* became the first large carrier to assume the role. Soon after, old *Saratoga* would likewise join the team as would several escort carriers. The defensive offensive was a 24-hour, seven-day-a-week affair.

During January 1945 *Enterprise* swept the sea north of Luzon and the waters of the China Sea hitting shore targets and shipping from Formosa to French Indo-China. After again replenishing at Ulithi, *Enterprise* returned in time to provide night and day coverage for the 16-17 February raids on Tokyo. And just as she had provided coverage for *Hornet* in April 1942 during the first attack on Tokyo, *Enterprise* was called upon again to cover the second Navy raid on the Japanese capital. Not

Enterprise obscured by smoke after being hit on 20 March 1945. USN

Firefighting on Enterprise *flight deck 20 March 1945. Note 5-inch guns ready for additional attacks.*   USN

Close-up view of damage to area just forward of the island, 20 March 1945.   USN

Damage to one of the 40mm guns mounts 20 March 1945. USN

all her time on this second raid was spent on defense as it had been in 1942. This time there would be occasion for *Enterprise* flyers to attack the city themselves.

Immediately after the Tokyo raid *Enterprise* took up station off the Marines' latest island objective—Iwo Jima. Arriving in time to support the initial landings on 19 February, *Enterprise* remained until 9 March at which time the issue had again been settled. An exceedingly high price tag, the lives of over 5,900 Marines and approximately 23,000 Japanese were expended in the fight for a land area less than 12 square miles. The battle on Iwo was grim evidence of what an invasion of the homeland would bring, but for the time being attention centered on preparing Iwo for use in the systematic bombing of Japan by B-29s. While supporting the Iwo operation the Big E set a record for having planes continuously in the air for 174 hours

from 23 February to 2 March. Initial planning called for *Enterprise* to share night coverage of Iwo with *Saratoga,* but *Sara* was badly wounded by bombs and planes of seven kamikazes on 21 February and the 23-year-old carrier originally laid down as a battlecruiser was out of the war.

By the end of the battle on Iwo Jima, Japanese kamikazes had already scored several notable successes. In addition to wounding *Franklin* and *Belleau Wood* in October 1944 and *Saratoga* in February 1945, the escort carriers *St. Lo* and *Bismarck Sea* had been sunk; *Bismarck Sea* on the same evening that *Saratoga* was struck. To the middle of March 1945 *Enterprise* crewmembers had seen the destructive power of the kamikaze but had not yet felt its sting. But a carrier cannot be within range of a constantly blowing "divine wind" for so long a time and expect to only hand out destruction and not receive in kind. The law of averages was about to catch up with *Enterprise.*

On 17 March *Enterprise* again took up her position after a short replenishment run to Ulithi and continued her night coverage while attacks were carried out against the Japanese home islands of Kyushu and Honshu and adjacent waters. On the 18th *Enterprise* antiaircraft fire downed several of the omnipresent kamikazes and enemy bombers, but one slipped through and dropped a "dud" bomb which damaged the flight deck and resulted in the death of one man. And, "friendly" antiaircraft gunfire from other ships in the formation came too close to the carrier and killed two 20mm gunners.

On the night of the 18th and early morning of the 19th Bill Martin's Avengers were heading for the Inland Sea of Japan. This was the deepest penetration at night for the *Enterprise* air group and although no confirmed sinkings occurred, the super-battleship *Yamato* and the carrier *Amagi* were hit.

On the morning of the 19th *Franklin* received the blows that yet cause Americans to flinch in dismay. Over 700 men were killed and 265 wounded. *Enterprise* was just over the horizon, but her men could hear the detonations and see the hugh black columns of smokes. Shortly, *Enterprise* crewmembers could see the damaged carrier as orders came for *Enterprise* to escort *Franklin* clear of the combat area. The going was slow and attacks continued, but at length *Franklin's* damage control party extinguished the flames; the carrier dropped its tow and worked up sufficient speed to carry herself to Pearl and then on to New York. Many aboard *Enterprise* felt great pain for *Franklin* and her men. It would have been bad enough just to hear about it; it was much worse to have to see it. But there would not be a protracted period to mourn for *Franklin.* The next day, 20 March 1945. *Enterprise* would again mourn her own.

As the American Fleet steamed off the Japanese homeland, enemy bombers and kamikazes came early and often. The routine each day while in the combat zone was the same: battle stations. When enemy planes were picked up on radar or spotted by the CAP, noise and vibration indicated *Enterprise* was working up to fighting speed (usually 25 knots or above). When the enemy planes appeared the guns began to fire, 5-inch first, then the 40s and finally the close range 20s and the ship began its wild turns. Those stationed on or near the fantail remember that they would have chosen almost any other place to be because the fantail literally bounced, shook and banged over the water during a high speed turn. Too, battle casualties were carried to the stern while a battle was in progress and respect for the dead notwithstanding, a stern approach by an enemy plane meant that living men in that area would have to hit the deck; on top of the dead if necessary. During the days of the defensive offensive it was often necessary.

On 20 March the enemy came early and for a while it appeared that the sky was raining kamikazes. Shooting was good, however, and no deck crashes occurred even though two planes hit the water less than 25 yards from *Enterprise* and two bombs struck even closer giving the ship a good rattling. But the major damage of the day did not come from enemy planes or bombs. Again, "friendly" antiaircraft fire came too close to *Enterprise* and a 5-inch shell burst just above the two quad 40 mounts forward of the island. Concussion and fragments from the shell killed seven men, wounded 30 and damaged fully-loaded Hellcats nearby. Within seconds gasoline fires from the Hellcats and exploding ordnance enveloped the carrier in flame and smoke. The pictures accompanying this chapter fully demonstrate the ship's plight in the first moments of her latest wound. The vast amount of smoke given off by the deck fires made the situation look worse than it was to other ships in the formation and there was relieved surprise to see the Big E still steaming in formation minutes later. Damage control soon had the fires under control and the ship continued in fighting trim and proved it by shooting down two more attackers. Still, damage was sufficient to force the carrier back to Ulithi for a week of repairs.

Returning to action on 5 April, *Enterprise* supported the Okinawa invasion until 11 April when again she was struck by a kamikaze. Just like the 18th, 19th and 20th of March, the skies were raining enemy planes on 11 April. Despite good shooting again by antiaircraft gunners, a suicider approached from the rear and hit the carrier near the two portside quad 40 mounts just off the hangar deck as the ship turned away from the flaming plane. The bomb from this plane missed the ship but hit the water so close that it had the effect of a torpedo. The ship's torpedo blister was penetrated, two generators were blown loose, several fuel tanks were destroyed, framing was bent, and the enemy plane's engine was embedded in the carrier's hull. Water entered the carrier and for several minutes the extent of the damage was not known. Even radar and other instruments were effected by the blast and as soon as all damages were reported it was obvious the carrier would have to head for repairs again. On the way to Ulithi on 12 April 1945 word came of Franklin D. Roosevelt's death, and what joy that existed in having a few days at Ulithi away from Okinawa was lost with the sad message reporting the president's passing.

Repair ships at Ulithi were becoming very familiar to *Enterprise* in the spring of 1945. Indeed, the repair ships were becoming well-known to the entire fleet. The period of the greatest loss in ships sunk and damaged in the history of the United States was that spent off the shores of Okinawa. During the fight for Okinawa the United States lost 30 ships sunk and 368 damaged. Few of the car-

The classic picture of Enterprise's *forward elevator being blown over 400 feet in the air by the explosion resulting from Kamikaze Tomi Zai's attack, 14 May 1945.* NA

riers escaped damage and casualties. Only the battleships (due to their armor) and cruisers (due to not being primary targets) escaped significant damage and casualties. Among combat ships the pain fell mostly on carriers (due to being primary targets) and destroyers and destroyer escorts (picket ships usually the first sighted by enemy pilots).

Operating again in waters around Okinawa by 6 May, *Enterprise* now flew patrols both day and night to guard against aerial counterattack. Battle stations were manned at all times and by this time there were very few men on board who were too new to appreciate the constant danger. No one needed to be told to hit the deck when the shooting started, no one needed to ask if they could leave their battle station even during a lengthy rain squall, and no one complained about being forever "buttoned up" while in the combat zone. Never were there complaints when *Enterprise* would pass close enough to another ship to see other crews sunbathing, exercising or relaxing on deck. *Enterprise* men had seen too much for too long and they knew why they were at GQ when newer ships with newer men commanded by newer officers were not.

It would not be correct to say that no *Enterprise* crewmember was lost because all were totally disciplined. Not so. On the 20th of March a young officer panicked and abandoned ship on his own orders and was lost. On another occasion a "hot-rod" tractor driver backed himself overboard at high speed, and at least two men were killed in their bunks when they should have been at GQ. Still, *Enterprise* veterans even today are proud of the fact that 99 percent of their crew was sufficiently disciplined not to complain about GQ and pleased that their veteran officers had the good sense to keep them there.

On the 11th of May 1945 *Bunker Hill,* operating close beside *Enterprise* was struck by two kamikazes while her flight deck was full of gassed and armed planes. The ensuing damage was similar to the *Franklin's* experience and when the fires were finally out, *Bunker Hill* counted 396 dead and 264 wounded. Like *Franklin, Bunker Hill* would be partially repaired and decommissioned in 1947, but neither of these severely damaged carriers would join their other World War II Essex-class sisters in the postwar modernization programs. These were the only two ships of the class not to be modernized.

At the time she was hit *Bunker Hill* was serving as the units' flagship and when incapacitated, Admiral Mitscher moved his flag to *Enterprise.* The Big E would have only three fighting days left in her combat career, but she would go out in style. Just as it was for her when the war started and for many months thereafter, she was the flagship again.

Action began early on the morning of 14 May 1945 with the appearance of enemy planes. Several were shot down before the sun had burned away all the morning mist, but at 0700 a smart-flying Japanese pilot in a bomb-laden Zero broke out of the scattered clouds and deftly placed his plane on the Big E's flight deck just behind the forward elevator. The plane disintegrated upon impact, but the bomb, engine and body of pilot Tomi Zai continued on into the forward elevator pit. There the engine and Tomi Zai stayed, but the detonation of the bomb sent the forward elevator over 400 feet into the air. Numerous pictures were taken from nearby ships to record these moments and the photographs show all angles of the spectacular explosion. The picture selected for use in this book carries the caption from Navy officialdom as "the" picture of the event.

Enterprise was well-prepared to receive Tomi Zai. Men were at battle stations, damage control was ready, the flight deck forward was clear except for two planes and all fires were under control in 17 minutes and were out in 30. Only 14 men were killed and 68 wounded; too many, of course, but better then the fates of Franklin, Bunker Hill, Saratoga, Intrepid and others. Fires out, Enterprise continued to battle other planes and she shot down two more.

Enterprise remained on station for two more days and in that time tried to patch her wounds. The list was removed from the bow as holes in the hull were covered and the water pumped out, but the flight deck was beyond the help of all but a major shipyard. From the forward elevator back to the island the wood and steel deck was raised approximately three to four feet and was broken through in several places. Planes could be recovered but could be flown off only by precariously moving them one at a time around the gaping hole that had been number one elevator to the starboard catapult. In a combat zone this condition was entirely unsatisfactory, and on 16 May Enterprise left the western Pacific never to return.

The Pacific war would continue for three months, but it was over for the Big E. On the 30th of May the carrier arrived to a rousing welcome at Pearl Harbor. This was only the first of warm and loud receptions she was to receive in the following months. After unloading some unneeded equipment and re-assigning a few men—ordnance had been dropped off at Ulithi—Enterprise departed for Bremerton and arrived on 7 June 1945. A few days later the carrier entered drydock for repairs to all her recent-

Enterprise *rides low at the bow as a result of taking on water after the Kamikaze crash. Note disfigured deck and damaged plane at bow.*

NA

Firefighting on the flight deck of Enterprise *just after the Kamikaze crash. Note impact point a few feet aft of the just-departed forward elevator.*
NA

ly incurred damage, another paint job, and the usual maintenance and overhaul. On 2 July 1945 Secretary of the Navy (soon to be the first Secretary of Defense) James E. Forrestal paid a visit to the Big E and saw for himself the damage within the great ship that from the first day of war had fought her way across the Pacific to downtown Tokyo.

While *Enterprise* was still in drydock, a lone B-29 carried an atomic bomb to Hiroshima on 6 August 1945 and on the 14th of that month the Japanese accepted unconditional surrender. The decision to use the bomb by new president Harry S. Truman saved numerous American lives. And in retrospect it saved many Japanese lives. Had the war not ended in August the main islands of the Japanese homeland would have been invaded and it is presumptuous to say that only a small number of Japanese lives would have been lost. For nearly four years the Japanese demonstrated they would fight to the end. There is no documented evidence to present that indicates the Battle of Japan would have been any different than Tarawa, Peleliu or Iwo Jima.

Part of damage below decks resulting from suicide crash.

Damage to quarters beneath impact area 14 May 1945.

Close-up view of damage to flight deck, 14 May 1945.   USN

Triumphant return to Pearl Harbor 30 May 1945.   NA

With her recent wounds quite apparent, Enterprise *arrives at Bremerton, Washington for overhaul and repair, June 1945.* USN

Secretary of the Navy James E. Forrestal inspects the forward elevator area of Enterprise *at Puget Sound Navy Yard 2 July 1945.* NA

CHAPTER NINE
Navy Day

By early September 1945 *Enterprise* was out of the Puget Sound Navy Yard. Never had she been more ready for a fight. Repaired, overhauled and armed to the teeth with an all-time high complement of medium range antiaircraft guns (56 forties), the Big E was ready for the Battle of Japan. Fortunately, however, most Japanese proved as disciplined in peace as in war· and the 14 August truce was not violated and formal surrender was signed on 2 September 1945. As of that date *Enterprise* was a warship without a war.

On 13 September *Enterprise* left Bremerton for Pearl Harbor via San Francisco and arrived at Pearl on 23 September. There the ship embarked Vice Admiral Frederick C. Sherman, Captain William L. Rees—her new captain—and 1,149 liberated POWs due for discharge. On 25 September the Big E was at sea again heading for New York City and the biggest Navy Day celebration ever held in the United States of America.

On the way to New York *Enterprise* was the flagship for a task force that included light carriers *Monterey* and *Bataan* and four battleships. While passing through the Panama Canal the celebration of the war's end began to take on formalities as the president of Panama and other dignitaries came aboard and traversed part of the Canal with the carrier. By the 16th of October the task force was within hours of New York City and 101 planes from *Enterprise*, *Monterey* and *Bataan* flew over America's primate city to herald the approach of the first 10 of 47 ships to participate in the big blowout. The overflight set the tone for the emotion that would find expression in the following two weeks as "the City" all but stopped to watch the aerial show.

New York newspapers had supplied considerable advance knowledge about the upcoming Navy Day celebration, and a review of the editions printed in those days leaves no doubt as to the magnitude of the impending celebration or the star of the event. After nearly four years of war America's most decorated warship was about to properly receive plaudits at center stage. That recognition in full had come to *Enterprise* is evident in the headlines and news accounts of New York's major newspapers. On the 16th of October the *New York Times* stated that *Enterprise* was "generally recognized as holding the greatest battle record in

American Naval history." On the 17th *The Sun* printed "The Pride of the Navy Comes Home in the Dawn's Early Light" over a front-page picture of the Big E as she moved through the early morning mist past the Manhatten skyline to her berth. A subheading on the same page read "*Montery* Leads Task Force: The Unsinkable Old *Enterprise* Trails Her Into Harbor As Bands Play." The *Times* informed readers "off eighty-fifth street will float the carrier *Enterprise*, the Navy's chief pride," and the *New York World-Telegram* carried the headline "The Big E, Fightin'est Carrier, In!"

During the two weeks *Enterprise* was in New York the newspapers and wire services seldom mentioned the Big E without adding adjectives such as "the mighty E," "the valiant carrier," etc. Too, there was almost constant mention that when battles were fought, *Enterprise* was there. In fact, some several battles were fought because *Enterprise* was there. But now instead of being the magnet that had drawn Japanese ships and planes to try and sink her, she drew media raves for her record and success. Of all the headlines, though, the favorite and one most appreciated by many was that of the *Daily News* on the 18th. The heading read "Home is the Sailor, Home from the Sea... (and then under a picture of the docked *Enterprise*) And the Hunter Home From the Kill."

When *Enterprise* arrived in the early morning hours of Wednesday the 17th photographers were out in force to record the event. Two Navy blimps, several private planes, tugs and private boats were loaded with photographers and a good-sized contingent was at Pier 26 on the North River at Beach Street to watch *Enterprise* tie up. Bands played, fire boats sprayed water and Waves and Red Cross girls gathered to cheer *Enterprise* crewmembers who in turn cheered the ladies. Thirty-five years after these moments just described most *Enterprise* veterans recall the fire boats first and do not even mention the Waves or Red Cross girls. However, the picture of the event contained herein seems to suggest that attention directed to dockside was well beyond the normal enthusiasm rendered to fire boats.

Festivities already begun in earnest on the 17th continued on Thursday the 18th when the Navy was presented the key to the city, Bob Hope traded wry remarks with Admiral Halsey and other Navy lumi-

All four classes of fast aircraft carriers to fight in the Pacific (except the one ship class of Wasp CV-7) are represented in this September 1945 photo at San Francisco. From left to right are Saratoga (Lexington-class), Enterprise (Yorktown-class), the second Hornet (Essex-class) and San Jacinto (Independence-class).

NA

naries at a welcoming dinner, the first of several parades was staged—and crewmen went ashore to investigate the amenities of "the Big Apple." Also on the 18th reporters climbed aboard the flagship and after taking pictures of the carrier and enjoying a brief tour, all went inside the Big E for a press conference. Admiral Sherman answered questions during the interview, but also used the occasion to speak on matters not forwarded by reporters. During one such commentary the Admiral referred to the near future need for the Navy to undergo a RIF (reduction in force) and in the course of the conversation said "Enterprise might be forced from the active list...I think she might well be preserved as a historical museum. I favor that."

Beginning on the afternoon of the 18th, visitors were allowed to come aboard and tour the flight deck and hangar deck of Enterprise. Other ships as they arrived also allowed visitors, and thousands of men, women and children trooped aboard. Even a contingent of West Point cadets came aboard. The war over, peace-time rivalry resurfaced and the West Pointers were "escorted" by a special detail to guard against the removal of souvenirs. Unquestionably, Enterprise was the main attraction and on board people talked with crewmembers, paid particular attention to the ship's guns and stood in awe before the bulkhead paintings recording the carrier's battle record. Long lines waited in good and bad weather to board the famous carrier and while waiting many had the occasion to observe the fantail whereon the raised letters spelling out ENTER-PRISE had been painted white. Little could they know then that only a few years later that nameplate would be the only remaining portion of the famous hull.

While the masses continued to climb aboard the victor of Midway and the Solomon Islands, other ships arrived in New York to participate in the activities. By Navy Day on Saturday 27 October, 47 ships would be present to trade salutes with President Truman. Joining Enterprise in the center ring of attention would be the battleship Missouri, representing the President's home state and the vessel (naturally) upon which the Japanese surrender had been accepted; the cruiser Augusta which had carried President Truman to the Potsdam Conference and upon which the Atlantic Charter had been signed in August 1941 by President Roosevelt; the new Battle Carrier Midway (CV-41), commissioned in October 1945 too late to fight in World War Two but still in commission in 1982; and the old battleship New York which had been the flagship of the American Squadron at the German surrender at Scapa Flow in 1918 and, ironically, the host ship in 1918 to then Crown-Prince and later Emperor Hirohito. For the old New York this Navy Day celebration would be her swan song as she would be among the first U.S. Navy capital ships to be discarded after the war. But for another capital ship this Navy Day would mark her debut. At the Brooklyn Navy Yard the second Battle Carrier was being readied for commissioning on Navy Day, the USS Franklin D. Roosevelt (CV-42). It would be her destiny to never fire a shot in anger, and in 1980 she would die in exactly the same spot as Enterprise at Kearny, New Jersey.

Beginning on the night of Friday 26 October the assembled naval vessels turned on their searchlights just after dark and provided New York City with a dazzling "Night of Lights." This half-hour display of sweeping lights continued on Saturday

With Enterprise *in forefront, ships of the Pacific Fleet steam toward the Panama Canal and East Coast ports for Navy Day.*
USN

Enterprise *passing through the Panama Canal October 1945.*

and Sunday evenings and added to the overall festive atmosphere of the final weekend. On Saturday morning the 27th the main events began with President Truman joining Mrs. Roosevelt for the commissioning ceremony of the carrier honoring her late husband. There followed a parade, a presidential speech on foreign affairs, lunch for the presidential party aboard the *Missouri,* and then President Truman took his place on destroyer *Renshaw* for the fleet review. The review lasted nearly two hours during the afternoon at which time 1200 planes flew continuously overhead and the president received 21 gun salutes from the 47 ships riding at anchor. In the absence of the usual 3-inch peacetime saluting guns, 5-inch guns did most of the honors and just before dark the president, most likely possessing a headache of the first magnitude, boarded a train to return to Washington.

It was estimated that four to six million people observed the Navy Day proceedings and many were still on hand at dusk when the *Enterprise* night fighter air group put on a show. The planes flew over the anchored ships in salute, flew over a second time with their lights on in a 'V' formation to signify victory and finally flew over in an 'E' formation to salute their own famous ship. The demonstration by the *Enterprise* air group and a dinner of the Navy League at the Waldorf-Astoria Hotel featuring Secretary of the Navy James Forrestal as speaker brought the historic weekend to a close. One cannot imagine a Navy Day celebration since 1945 or at some time in the future that could possibly match the pagentry and emotional exuberance of the event just described. Navy Day 27 October 1945 easily lived up to its ballyhooed expectations and it provided a perfect setting for the curtain call of America's most notable World War Two warship, *Enterprise.*

The days of honors and recognition over, *Enterprise* departed New York for the Boston Navy Yard to have her hangar deck transformed into a large bunk room. Along with numerous other carriers, *Enterprise* participated in the 'Magic Carpet' operation which entailed the return of U.S. servicemen from Europe. Between November 1945 and the middle of January 1946 *Enterprise* transported over 10,000 troops from Europe back to the United States. The two round trips completed, *Enterprise* had rendered final service to her country.

On the way to New York City sailors take advantage of the warm sun on the flight deck of **Enterprise.** *Planes are Hellcats and Avengers.*

USN-Leahy Collection

-92-

At night planes were moved to the flight deck so cots could be placed on the hangar deck to make sleeping quarters for the 1,149 former POWs being returned to the United States aboard Enterprise.

New York City's famous skyline forms a picturesque background for the Enterprise *as she moves through the early morning Manhattan mists 17 October 1945.*

Vice Admiral Frederick L. Sherman (left) and Captain W.L. Rees stand with the admiral's pet dog "Wags" on the flight deck of the Enterprise. "Wags and his master were survivors of Lexington's sinking in the Coral Sea in May 1942.
USN-Leahy Collection

Red Cross workers and waves exchange greetings with Enterprise crewmembers as the carrier is secured to the dock.　USN-Leahy Collection

The crew of the Enterprise *lines the flight deck and exchanges salutes with President Truman.*

Navy Day on Saturday 27 October 1945. From left to right are Enterprise, *the new* Midway, *cruiser* Augusta, *cruiser* Boise *and cruiser* Columbus.

Blimps lazily bid goodnight to warships of the U.S. Fleet at the close of the biggest Navy Day celebration in New York history. Enterprise is in the foreground and her planes (above) are beginning their fly-over.

USN-Leahy Collection

CHAPTER TEN
The Final Battle

When Vice Admiral Frederick Sherman told New York City and wire service reporters in October 1945 that he expected *Enterprise* to be preserved as a historical museum, he was not close to being the first to forward or support the idea. Men aboard the Big E and many aboard other ships who fought beside the carrier at Eastern Solomon's, Santa Cruz, Guadalcanal and other battles knew in 1943 that *Enterprise* was unique in the annals of naval history. By late 1944 the need for censorship had diminished sufficiently to allow news stories to identify ships by name and belatedly the story of the valiant carrier began to be told to the American people. As mentioned earlier, Eugene Burn's book *Then There Was One* was published in 1944. That book and an excellent article in the 1 September 1945 *Saturday Evening Post* by Charles Rawlings recounting the carrier's battle history and May 1945 encounter with kamikaze Tomi Zai documented the fame that brought *Enterprise* official and unofficial recognition in the closing days of the war. The tremendous reception by the city of New York and the glowing articles in that city's newspapers concerning the courageous ship during the Navy Day celebration was crowned on 1 November 1945 when President Harry S. Truman approved the following letter written to him by Secretary of the Navy James Forrestal.

Time has accomplished what the enemy failed to do in four years of desperate and costly effort; the USS ENTERPRISE *must be taken out of service because modern planes cannot be flown in combat from her flight deck.*

The ship was the heart of the Fleet when the war was going badly for us. The names of more than a score of battles are in her record of service and she has survived many attacks. She made our first attack on Japanese territory at the Marshalls and Gilberts in February of 1942, she flew the flag of Admiral (then Rear Admiral) Spruance in the Battle of Midway, one of the decisive battles of history, and after the Hornet was lost in the battle of the Santa Cruz Islands the Enterprise *was our only carrier in the Pacific. Her crew proudly proclaimed that it was* ENTERPRISE *against Japan and steamed into the Battle of Guadalcanal. Her squadrons shot down nearly a thousand of the enemy's planes and sank seventy-four of his ships.*

The men who fought her love this ship. It would grieve me to put my name to the document which would consign her to be broken up for scrap.

I believe, Mr. President, that the ENTERPRISE *should be returned permanently to some proper place as a visible symbol of American valor and tenacity in war, and of our will to fight all enemies who assail us, and I request your approval of this proposal.*

This recognition and letter of recommendation seemingly assured the preservation of the United State's most decorated ship to fight through World War Two. But it was not to be.

After her Magic Carpet voyages in November-December 1945 and January 1946 *Enterprise* rested at Bayonne, New Jersey for the following 12 years. Her commission pennant was lowered on 17 February 1947, and the last members of her crew and last captain, Commander Lewis F. Davis, left the ship on that date. Even though it was known she could not be modernized to land the heavy jet planes that by the early 1950s had succeeded propeller-driven craft, the Big E was still in reserve as a member of the Atlantic Reserve Fleet. Upkeep on the carrier, however, was minimal. *Enterprise,* like other mothballed ships, received attention to keep her safe from taking on water and from catching fire, but funding and personnel limitations allowed no further care. In those years she became dirty and in need of paint.

Despite all her unmet needs, there was to be one last bright moment for the carrier. In 1956 the third reunion of the *Enterprise* Association was held at the Astor Hotel in New York City. Over 350 of her former crewmembers attended and the highlight of the reunion was a visit to the ship at Bayonne. If *Enterprise* did indeed possess a soul, this moment must have been the most memorable for her.

Time not spent aboard the carrier or socializing during the 1956 reunion was devoted to discussing preservation plans for *Enterprise* as a national monument. In 1949 a serious effort was made by the San Francisco Museum of Science and Industry to have the *Enterprise* assigned and berthed at the U.S. Naval Station, Treasure Island, San Francisco, California. Correspondence from the Museum's director, Commander Howard M. McKinley (Ret.), recognized the greatness of the *Enterprise* and pro-

posed to use the ship as a living memorial of World War Two and for appropriate displays, shops for occupational and industrial therapy, school programs, electrical and mechanical engineering instruction, lecture rooms, theatre, library, print shop for publication of bulletins and pamphlets, for use as a standby electrical plant for Treasure Island and as a research laboratory for the Pacific area. Finally, Commander McKinley recognized the value of *Enterprise* for recruitment purposes. Although honorary trustees of the Museum included such luminaries as General Hap Arnold and Admiral Nimitz, the request to the Secretary of the Navy was declined because the Navy would have to incur the expense of moving *Enterprise* to San Francisco and maintaining the ship after she got there. The San Francisco venture having failed, the *Enterprise* Association agreed in 1956 to further discuss preservation plans at the 1957 San Diego, California meeting. However, the 1956 meeting had just ended when Secretary of the Navy Thomas S. Gates released a long list of ship's names the Navy could no longer afford to maintain even in mothball status and would be sold for scrap. *Enterprise* was on the list.

In 1956 *Enterprise* was only 18 years old from time of commissioning and 20 years old from time of launching, but the Big E was very old for her age. She was ancient in terms of experience, old in wear and repair, obsolete in technology and tired from overwork. She was not alone. Even the majority of modern battleships authorized in the massive 1938 congressional allocations were out-of-date and the Big E's old friends *South Dakota, Washington, North Carolina, Alabama* and numerous former attending cruisers and destroyers were scheduled for dismantling between 1956 and the early '60s. Although caught by surprise at the Navy Department's announcement, the *Enterprise* Association executive board moved immediately to save their ship.

Help was soon in coming. Joe Morchouser, a writer for *Look,* wrote an outstanding article in the 5 March 1957 edition of the magazine and suggested readers write their congressmen to support the project. The article contained several favorable quotes concerning the preservation of the carrier by the project's chairman and old friend of *Enterprise,* Admiral Bill Halsey. Once again the carrier and the man who took her to war 10 days before the Pearl Harbor attack and rode her through the darkest days of the war were reunited. Halsey, remembering especially the occasion when the Big E came up over the horizon just in time to make the difference at Santa Cruz in October 1942, set off vigorously to repay his old flagship. He appeared on television's *I've Got a Secret,* was interviewed on the *Mike Wallace Show* and did numerous other media interviews and newspaper articles. His effort

plus those of others such as a program by Navy Log contributed to national recognition of the historical endeavor.

The results of the campaign brought forth fruit when resolutions were presented in both houses of congress. On 22 May 1957 Senator Warren G. Magnuson introduced S.J. Resolution 96 for the establishment of the USS *Enterprise* as a national shrine in the District of Columbia. In his introductory remarks Senator Magnuson recalled his own experiences in the Navy and with *Enterprise.* He noted "*Enterprise*...has been the subject of many motion pictures and many naval stories...is, of course, one of the greatest ships in the history of the entire Navy...Let me add that the chevrons on her stack finally required so much space that sometimes we thought we might have to raise her stack a little." In the House of Representatives, chairman of the House Armed Services Committee Carl Vinson (for whom nuclear aircraft carrier CVN-70 was named in recognition of Vinson's 50 years of support for naval needs) asked for unanimous consent for the immediate consideration of S.J. Resolution 96 on 21 August 1957 and after lauding her deeds commented "it seems appropriate that the *Enterprise* be selected for memorial purposes." The following resolution was approved and signed by President Dwight D. Eisenhower (for whom nuclear carrier CVN-69 is named) on 28 August 1957.

> Whereas the U.S.S. Enterprise, *after 20 years of outstanding service in the United States Navy, has been declared to be obsolete by reason of having outlived its military usefulness; and*
>
> Whereas the U.S.S. Enterprise *was known as the fightingest carrier in the fleet during World War II, during which time it accumulated 18 of 22 possible combat stars for carriers in the Pacific area; and*
>
> Whereas the U.S.S. Enterprise *at one period during World War II was the only aircraft carrier operating in the Pacific; and*
>
> Whereas, *although reported by the Japanese to be sunk 7 times, the* U.S.S. Enterprise *succeeded in accounting for 911 Japanese aircraft, 71 enemy ships sunk by her pilots, and another 192 ships damaged or probably sunk; and*
>
> Whereas the U.S.S. Enterprise *was called the Galloping Ghost of the Oahu Coast by Fleet Adm. William F. Halsey, Jr., and during the early days of World War II symbolized the American resistance against a foe advancing with seemingly overwhelming strength: Now, therefore be it*
>
> Resolved, etc., *That subject to the conditions hereafter prescribed, at such time as the* U.S.S. Enterprise *is released by the United States and acquired by the* Enterprise Association *and its distinguished leader, Fleet Adm. William F. Halsey, United States Navy (retired), it may be berthed at, or in the vicinity of, the Nation's Capital as a memorial museum to be supported and maintained by private funds at no expense to the United States or the*

Government of the District of Columbia.

Sec. 2. In furtherance of the purposes of this act, the Secretary of the Navy is authorized to transfer the Enterprise to the Enterprise Association upon conditions (1) that a showing satisfactory to the Secretary of the Navy that the association is in a suitable position financially, or will be in a suitable position financially, to move, repair, renovate, berth, prepare for display, maintain, and administer such vessel satisfactorily and in the public interest for purposes of this act; (2) that a site for berthing the vessel with adequate land approach facilities is approved (a) by the Secretary of the Navy, the National Capital Planning Commission and the Secretary of Commerce and (b) if such site is within or adjacent to areas under their jurisdiction, also by the Secretary of the Interior, the Fine Arts Commission, and the Board of Commissioners of the District of Columbia; (3) that the Enterprise will not be operated for profit above necessary operating and maintenance costs.

Sec. 3. If the conditions described in section 2 are not met within 6 months of the date of enactment of this act, the Secretary of the Navy may dispose of the U.S.S. Enterprise in accordance with law.

Enterprise in drydock at Bayonne, New Jersey, 1953.   NA

The site selected for berthing the *Enterprise* was to be on the Potomac River near the Washington Monument. This, however, is as far as details for the preservation were to go. The seeds of failure for the project were contained within the congressional resolution: (1) only six months were allocated for raising necessary funds, and (2) total financial responsibility fell upon the *Enterprise* Association. Once it was determined that costs for movement, repair, renovation, berthing, preparation for display, maintenance and administration would approximate two million dollars, Admiral Halsey and the executive board of the Association knew their hopes and plans were doomed.

The final battle was over almost as soon as it began. In retrospect there seem to have been four major reasons why the great carrier was lost. First, *Enterprise* was the first major World War Two warship to be presented to the American Public and congress as a national memorial museum.[1] Being first was nothing new to *Enterprise* as she had won several pre-war competitions, was the first carrier during the war to engage the enemy, was the first

[1] USS *Texas* became a state museum in 1948.

Enterprise *Tower at the Navy and Marine Corps football stadium Annapolis, Maryland. Note dedicatory plaque honoring* Enterprise *at the base of the Elevator Tower.*   Thomas Lake, NAAA

American ship to sink a Japanese combat vessel, was first to attack Japanese territory, was first to win the Presidential Unit Citation, was the first and only carrier to win the Navy Unit Commendation in World War Two, was the Navy's first night operations fleet carrier and was first in battle star's awarded. This time, however, it was not to her advantage to be first. Her precedent was through uncharted waters and *Enterprise* was not to be as effective in peace as she had been in war.

Secondly, the timing was not good. In many ways 1957 was too soon to offer *Enterprise* as a museum. World War Two was only 12 years past, many of the ships that sailed and fought in the Pacific were still in service and the uniqueness of this one ship could not be fully apreciated at that time in a historical context. While being too soon, 1957 was also too late. Sociologists would note the middle class society of the United States in 1957 and point to their studies that indicate middle class societies to be future-oriented. Being future-oriented would consign historical objects such as *Enterprise* to a long distant, perhaps irrelevant past. And in October 1957 the Soviet Union placed into space the first Sputnik, and the American people and their government suddenly became very future-oriented. *Enterprise* could not fight potential battles of the future and after October 1957 it became extremely difficult to direct attention to her.

The third reason was the extremely short time of six months to accomplish the requirements of the fourth reason, finances. In 1957 two million dollars was a lot more money than two million dollars in 1982. That congress could not help is somewhat understandable. Budgets were tight even before the alarm caused by Sputnik and that event signaled the need for an expanded budget for research, a new Navy to meet a new threat, new military equipment, and even new funding for secondary schools and colleges to enhance the teaching of science, math and related disciplines. And on the horizon was the need for new money to meet social problems. Whereas only 10 percent of the American population in 1980 was defined as living in poverty, in 1957 the corresponding figure was close to 30 percent. Certainly, Admiral Halsey could not finance the project on his retirement pay and the former crewmembers of the ship in 1957 were mostly just getting started in their post-war occupations. For many of the former crew there was barely enough money to care for themselves and their families. Finally, *Enterprise* was lost because these men did not have time to leave their jobs, solicit large contributions and follow up on the many contacts inherent in such an effort. Even if contacted, it must be noted, many Navy-related businesses and industries were not riding good economic waves in 1957.

In later years people interested in preserving other ships noted the problems in the effort to save *Enterprise* and profited from her experience. Too, they were inspired by the knowledge that if *Enterprise* could be lost, any and all other ships were in jeopardy.

With the realization of the hopelessness of raising the necessary funds for *Enterprise* in the short time alloted, a meeting was held by the executive board of the Association and Secretary of the Navy Gates. Secretary Gates had been and continued to be cooperative with and sympathetic to the preservation project, but he was in a bind in that he had to continue spending funds to maintain *Enterprise* in reserve status when he needed the money to support the operational fleet. He could not dispose of the carrier because of the congressional resolution and therefore a compromise was agreed upon by the Secretary and the Association for an alternate memorial. In consideration of the Association's abandoning its drive to preserve the ship, Secretary Gates agreed to (1) name the first nuclear aircraft carrier (CVN-65) *Enterprise*; (2) allow the Association to have the Elevator Tower at the new Navy-Marine Corps Stadium being built at Annapolis at a reduced price donation of $10,000; and (3) give to the Association any parts from the Big E that would be appropriate to become part of the alternate

memorial to the carrier. In 1960 the world's first nuclear carrier became the eighth *Enterprise* and the new football stadium at Annapolis is served by *Enterprise* Tower with two plaques embedded in the concrete Tower to commemorate the carrier. However, the original agreement to place the tripod mast of the carrier at the top of the Tower to fly the National Ensign was not honored. Architects later complained that the steel mast would require periodic maintenance and part of the intent of building a concrete stadium was to eliminate maintenance. Too, it was said that the mast was not in keeping with the overall design of the stadium. All this was most unfortunate. No other part of the great carrier was as distinctive as the mast. Nice as they are, the two plaques in the Tower will never convey the aura of the carrier that would have emanated from viewing the National Ensign above the 36-foot high mast.

During the campaign to save *Enterprise,* the Association asked the Navy to nominate an author to write a book on the ship and Commander Edward P. Stafford was appointed. The result was *The Big E* published by Random House which is and forever will be the definitive literary work concerning the *Enterprise.* The Association yet owns a percentage of the author's royalties and any movie or television rights that might be sold. Sale of

The distinctive tripod mast that was supposed to be placed on top of the Enterprise *Tower at Annapolis lying on deck.*

Hoffmann Collection

Enterprise *at Kearny, Fall 1958.*

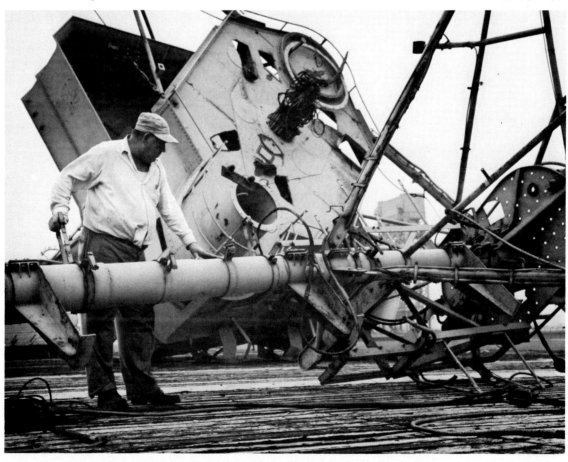

Removal of mast from the deck to the yard signaled the beginning of demolition.

copies of *The Big E,* sale of picture frame kits consisting of four pieces of wood taken from the Enterprise's flight deck, and sale of individual shares paid the $10,000 pledge for the *Enterprise* Tower at Annapolis.

The campaign over, the compromise struck and agreements in place for an alternate memorial, Secretary Gates was free to dispose of the carrier. On 1 July 1958 *Enterprise* was sold to Lipsett, Incorporated for the sum of $561,333, a dollar figure that would not pay for a single fighter aboard the present *Enterprise.*

THE DISMANTLING

In the fall of 1958 *Enterprise* was moved from the Brooklyn Navy Yard, where she had been tied up beside the new carrier *Independence* (CV-62), to her last port of call, Kearny, New Jersey on the Hackensack River. Her new owners, Lipsett, were not new to the ship dismantling business. Under the direction of W. Henry Hoffmann the company had been responsible for taking apart the 60,000-ton French liner *Normandie* which had burned and capsized in New York harbor during the war. In 1948 the company acquired the old battleships *New Mexico, Idaho* and *Wyoming* for dismantling and later added to their credit the famous cruiser *Augusta* upon whose decks the Atlantic Charter had been

Architect of the demolition of Enterprise, *Mr. Henry Hoffmann.* United Technologies

signed. In later years the Kearny company would change hands and today is known as River Terminal Development Company. Since 1958 several well-known aircraft carriers have been dismantled at Kearny: *Essex, Wasp, Boxer, Antietam* and the carrier that was commissioned during the 1945 Navy Day ceremonies, USS *Franklin D. Roosevelt.* But again, *Enterprise* would register a first. She was the first fleet carrier of her size to be dismantled while still in the water.

It was fortunate for naval history that the man in charge of the destruction of *Enterprise* was Henry Hoffmann. Already somewhat of a legend among his peers due to his successful work on the *Normandie,* Hoffmann also directed the scrapping of the battleships and cruiser mentioned above and was instrumental in the demolition of historical structures other than ships such as the Singer Building and Penn Station. A self-taught engineer, Hoffmann began his career as a foreman during construction of part of the New York City subway system in the late 1920s and early 1930s. At night he would study engineering from library sources and apply his learning the following day on the job. His connection between engineering and ships was natural because he was a navy man. During World War One Hoffmann saw considerable action...in the German Navy. Two ships were blown from under him during the war and after one such experience he had to travel all the way to South America before finding passage back to Germany. After a stint of fighting against the communists in the Russian Civil War, a tour in the Norwegian Merchant Marine and other adventures he made his way to the United States.

Hoffmann's naval experience never left him. He understood a man's feeling for ships and he understood a man's emotion for the ship upon which he had served. Even though he did not serve aboard *Enterprise,* Hoffmann was fascinated by the carrier. He knew her battle record and greatness and because of his appreciation of *Enterprise* and his own experience in the German Navy, part of what survives of the ship today does so because of him.

When *Enterprise* arrived at Kearny, Hoffmann immediately began his plan of destruction, but he also spent time wrestling within himself about the dismantling of such a historic vessel. Within himself it was a struggle only partially resolved. His ambivalence was divided by thoughts on one hand that the United States did not fully appreciate its history and should not be so unsentimental in regard to the carrier that symbolized some of the country's finest hours in the Pacific war. On the other hand Hoffmann realized *Enterprise* was an instrument of destruction and that she had been extremely successful in her destructive role and perhaps it was then best to observe the biblical

The ransacked, neglected hangar deck of Enterprise, *Fall 1958.*   Hoffmann Collection

Flight crew ready room within Enterprise, *1958.*   Hoffmann Collection

passage of pounding swords into plowshares. Indeed, ideals were to be fought for, but then death and her tools were to be forgotten. So with partial resolution he turned to the job of destruction with an attitude that *Enterprise* had accomplished in high fashion the mission for which she had been built and he adopted the attitude of the Wall Street Journal editorial that commented "*Enterprise*...has no need for sad requiem or sentimental tear. Lipsetts torches won't destroy her."

During the days of the carrier's birth at Newport News in the middle 1930s, unexpected problems arose and during the days of her death in 1959 there were others. The first problem was a continuing one. Being the first large carrier to be dismantled while still afloat there was always the problem that the ship would capsize or break apart unexpectedly. Such an event would be costly both in terms of injury and cost. Secondly, fears were that a storm and/or high water would tear the ship away from her moorings at Kearny and that the Big E might strike again. Citizens crossing the downriver bridge no doubt cast a wary eye toward the carrier on days when high winds blew just to be sure they would not be among the ship's last victims. And originally, the plan of destruction was to take only six months, but the same somewhat sluggish economy that helped prevent the carrier's preservation now held prices for scrap metal at a level that would delay demolition.

At Kearny, Fall 1958.   Hoffman Collection

Delay in demolition was a blessing for the *Enterprise* Association. Although the Navy had removed radar installations, guns and numerous other items from the ship before it was sold, portions of the wooden flight deck had not been removed for the picture frames to be sold by the Association to pay the Annapolis *Enterprise* Tower pledge. Arrangements were made with Mr. Hoffmann by the Association to obtain the decking, but when the several former crewmembers arrived at Kearny to pick up the planks they found that industrious workmen at the yard had already burned the pile set aside for the Association. Hoffmann endeared himself to the former *Enterprise* crewmembers by immediately requisitioning a special saw and within minutes he had 50 employees of the company on deck to pull up another pile of lumber. On this and other occasions Hoffmann bent rules to accommodate former crewmembers. When Bill Ray, now of the *Winston-Salem Journal & Sentinel*, drove from North Carolina to catch one last view of his old ship, Hoffmann took the time to escort Ray through the vessel. On these and other occasions Hoffmann went the second mile for members of the Association, and later he went the second mile for the ship itself.

By the spring of 1959 the price of scrap metal was such that the demolition could get underway in earnest. In order that the carrier could pass under several bridges on the way to Kearny, the mast had been removed and placed on the flight deck before the ship was moved from New York City. At Kearny the first portion of the ship to go was the large island and bridge structure. The wooden flight deck planking was one of the few parts of the ship that could not be salvaged and was therefore burned. To continually maintain a balance that would not cause the ship to capsize or break up, precise engineering calculations were made by Hoffmann and the plan of destruction was dictated by these considerations. The two biggest challenges in this process were removal of the 140-foot non-buoyant bow and the four shafts and propellers, each weighing 39 tons. The carrier was cut away on both ends, her innards removed by crane and finally her keel was winched onto a beaching area. The steel, copper, brass and aluminum were carried away by railroad cars, generators and refrigerators marketed, and by March 1960 all was finished. *Enterprise* was gone.

Even though the keel of the ship was not consumed until March 1960, as a distinctive structure *Enterprise* was gone by the end of 1959. Just as 1959 was the year of death for the famous carrier, so was it also the year of death for her most famous mentor, friend and protector, Fleet Admiral William F. Halsey. *Enterprise* and Halsey, a great team in battle and victory, together finally in death.

Removal of Douglas fir planking via jackhammer. Most of the decking was burned but some souvenir blocks remain today.
Hoffmann Collection

A crane lifts a section from the aft portion of the carrier.
Hoffmann Collection

Winter 1959. Island, flight deck and fantail structures are gone.

Cutting away the bow, Winter 1959.

CHAPTER ELEVEN
Legacy

The term "legacy" is defined as something passed from one generation to succeeding generations. Further, the term implies that something from the past now belongs to the present and will belong to the future. The legacy of *Enterprise* was the inheritance of a famous name and tradition that she honored in the days she carried the name and then passed on an even greater tradition to the warship that carries the name today. In view of her performance during World War Two, it is doubtful that anymore appropriate name could have been given to CV-6 as "*Enterprise*" means a "bold undertaking or venture with some risk."

THE ENTERPRISE HERITAGE

Six vessels of the U.S. Navy carried the name *Enterprise* before it was inherited by CV-6. The first *Enterprise* was originally a British supply sloop captured 18 May 1775 and put into use on Lake Champlain. Armed with only 12 four-pounders, the sloop battled stronger British units twice and contributed to the Revolutionary cause. She was run aground on 7 July 1777 and burned to avoid capture. The second *Enterprise,* a schooner of eight guns, was purchased 20 December 1776 and served the Continental cause in Chesapeake Bay. Full information on the life and service of this vessel is not known but indications are that she was returned intact to the Maryland Council of Safety no later than February 1777.

The third ship of the U.S. Navy named *Enterprise* was the one that began in earnest to establish the tradition maintained so well by CV-6. Commanded during her career by such illustrious naval officers as Lt. Stephen Decatur, Jr., Lt. William Burrows, David Porter and Isaac Hull she fought constantly against French privateers during the Quasi-War with France (1799-1801), the Barbary pirates, the British during the War of 1812, and on one occasion she took on a flotilla of Spanish gunboats (1806). During her 24-year existence "Lucky Little *Enterprise*" as she was called, captured 27 ships, liberated at least 12 American vessels, defeated the famous British ship *Boxer* and fought beside *Constitution* to capture the Tripolitan ketch which was renamed *Intrepid*. A landing party from "Lucky"

under the command of Decatur burned the captured Philadelphia in Tripoli harbor, and on this and other occasions raiding parties from the ship were known for raising a degree of havoc that would have made more contemporary *Enterprise* crewmen even more proud of their association with their ship's name. "Lucky's" luck ran out on 9 July 1823 and her long career ended when she was stranded and broke up in the West Indies. Even so, no crewmember was lost. It has been said of her that she "never met with a reverse, nor a serious mishap; never failed to capture any antagonist with whom she joined issue in battle, and when forced to escape from absolutely overwhelming odds, was able to out-distance her pursuers, in one case only after a chase of 70 hours."

The fourth *Enterprise*, a 10-gun schooner, served from 1831 until final decommissioning in 1844. The fifth ship served from 1879 to 1909 and was steam-powered with auxiliary sailpower. Before ending her days as a training ship she sailed around the world (1883-1886) on a hydrographic survey that added considerably to the knowledge of ocean depths and currents. The sixth *Enterprise* was originally a private yacht which served in a non-commissioned status during World War One as a patrol motorboat.

The seventh *Enterprise* was the carrier CV-6 to which this writing has been directed. The great carrier received the legacy of the *Enterprise* name, lived up to its heritage, embellished it, and then passed the tradition on to the eighth *Enterprise* which is the contemporary nuclear-powered aircraft carrier CVN-65. The world's first nuclear carrier was launched 24 December 1960 at the same yard that built her predecessor, Newport News Shipbuilding and Drydock Company. Commissioned on 25 November 1961 the 1,123-foot-long, 85,350-ton carrier first distinguished herself by exceeding expectations during her shakedown trials. From 1965 to 1967 warplanes rose repeatedly from her flight deck in the Pacific to fight yet another enemy of the United States.

Just as the World War Two *Enterprise* knew the pain of losing pilots and suffering damage to itself, it has been the same with the latest *Enterprise*. On its first sortie in the Vietnamese conflict on 2 December 1965, CVN-65 launched 118 times. Two

PRESIDENTIAL UNIT CITATION
DEC. 7ᵗʰ 1941   NOV. 15ᵗʰ 1942

1942	ACTION AGAINST JAPAN'S FORCES			
FEB. 1	GILBERT AND MARSHALL ISLANDS RAID	8	★4	36
FEB. 24	WAKE ISLAND RAID	1	★	3
MAR. 4	MARCUS ISLAND RAID		★	
APRIL 18	DOOLITTLE TOKYO RAID			
JUNE 4-6	BATTLE OF MIDWAY	2	4	9
AUG. 7-9	OCCUPATION OF GUADALCANAL		★	13
AUG. 24	BATTLE OF STEWART ISLANDS	1		44
OCT. 26	BATTLE OF SANTA CRUZ ISLANDS		3	63
NOV. 14-15	BATTLE OF SOLOMON ISLANDS	15	★4	17
	(MINOR ENGAGEMENTS NOT INCLUDED) TOTAL	27	16	185
	★ DESTRUCTIONS OF SHORE INSTALLATIONS			

DEC 7-1941 TO SEPT. 29⁴	AIR GROUP SIX					
	VB-6	VF-6	VS-6	VT-6	VB-3 VS-5	VT-3
SEPT. 30/42 TO NOV. 15.42	AIR GROUP TEN					
	VB 10	VF-10	VS 10	VT-10	VB 20	

U.S.S. Enterprise
"The Big E"

NIGHT AIR GROUP 90

OPERATIONS AS A NIGHT CARRIER
DATE . . . . DEC. 24 1944 ᵗᵒ MAY 31 1945 . . . . . ACTION

Jan. 7-8	SUPPORTING LUZON LANDINGS
	LUZON AIRFIELDS
Jan. 12	FRENCH-INDO-CHINA CAMRANH-BAY
	CAPE HIRONDELLES SAIGON
Jan. 15	PRATAS REEF
Jan. 16	HONG KONG CANTON
Jan. 20-22	FORMOSA AIRFIELDS KIIRUN HARBOR
Jan. 22	OKINAWA
Feb. 16-17	TOKYO *First Carrier Strikes*
Feb. 19-March 9	SUPPORTING IWO-JIMA LANDINGS
	IWO-JIMA HANA-JIMA CHICHI-JIMA
March 18-21	KYUSHU *First Carrier Strikes*
	INLAND SEA KYUSHU and SHIKOKU *Airfields* KOBE
April 7-12	SUPPORTING OKINAWA LANDINGS
	OKINAWA SAKISHIMA-GUNTO AMAMI-GUNTO
May 6-11	AMAMI-GUNTO DAITO-GUNTO
May 11-14	KYUSHU and SHIKOKU AIRFIELDS

TOTAL *NIGHT* SORTIES 1022

War record of the Big E.

NA

ON *against* JAPAN
5. 1942 TO DECEMBER 24, 1944

ACTION	JAPANESE LOSSES			
	SHIPS SUNK	SHIPS DAMAGED	PLANES DESTROYED	PLANES (IN AIR)
RENNELL ISLAND			11	
T ISLAND OCCUPATION			3	*
LFIN ATOLL RAID	3	8	14	*
HALL OCCUPATION		4	12	A
ISLANDS RAID	10	28	75	*
T RAID			1	*
WOLEAI (YAP) RAID	3	20	29	*
A OCCUPATION			81	*
SLANDS RAID		5	23	*
NAS ISLANDS OCCUPATION	3	2	39	*
PHILIPPINE SEA		3	32	
ISLAND RAID	3	4		*
ATION + PALAU				*
I SHOTO RAID	15	18	14	*
OSA RAID	4	13	45	*
ATION LEYTE ISLAND	2	9	152	*
PHILIPPINE SEA 2	3	18	4	
NE ISLANDS RAIDS	6	17	130	*
TOTALS	**52**	**150**	**664**	

OUP 10	VB-10	VF-10	VS 10	VT-10
UP 6	VB-6	VF-2	VT 6	
UP 10	VB-10	VF-10	VT-10	VF N 10
UP 20	VB-20	VF-20	VT-20	VF N 20

planes did not return that day, the first of many that would not. And on 14 January 1969, CVN-65 incurred a flight deck accident which killed 27 men and injured 65. The accident set off nine bombs and did tremendous damage, but bad as it was that accident has been helpful to proponents of nuclear aircraft carriers in modern war. The damage to *Enterprise* was estimated to be equal to the destructive force of six anti-ship missles. Despite her damage, CVN-65 could have been operational within hours and her overall effectiveness was not diminished.

The French have a saying that "the more things change, the more they stay the same." The quotation has application to the *Enterprise* heritage. Early in the Vietnamese conflict on 12 December 1965 the contemporary *Enterprise* established a combat record with 165 sorties in one day; not as many as the 236 the World War Two *Enterprise* flew off when she established a record on 7 August 1942, but still an interesting coincidence. And aboard another carrier, *Kitty Hawk* (CV-63), Lt. Commander Jim Flatley, son of the late Vice Admiral Jimmy Flatley, an ace who flew from the World War Two *Enterprise,* became on 1 April 1969 only the fourth pilot in U.S. naval history to record 1,000 landings on aircraft carriers as he completed his 150th combat mission over Vietnam. And presently (1982) Jim Flatley, like his late father, is an admiral.

The combat legacy of the World War Two *Enterprise* is too long to list in total, but before leaving the subject it must be mentioned that during the Pacific War two destroyers were named for *Enterprise* pilots who flew into the battle over Pearl Harbor and were lost: DE *Menges* 320 and DE *Willis* 395. Too, many of the men whose names were so closely associated with CV-6 have been honored by having ships named for them: DLG *Halsey*, a guided missile frigate in July 1963; a new class of 30 destroyers named after Admiral Raymond A. Spruance in the 1970s; and in 1980 a new cruiser named for Admiral John Crommelin and his four brothers.

Finally, fans of the television program *Star Trek* and football fans who crane their necks to watch one of the Goodyear blimps should know that the "*Enterprise*" name used by both is one of the several historic names dating from the revolutionary period of American history that have been and no doubt will continue to be used in the U.S. Navy because ships of succeeding generations have carried on their original fame and heritage. Among the famous names used along with *Enterprise* are *Essex, Hornet, Intrepid, Wasp* and *Columbia*.

ENTERPRISE CV-6:
HER HISTORICAL RECORD
AND MEMORIALS

Even though *Enterprise* CV-6 has been gone for nearly a quarter century, still existing in 1982 is her record, her decorations and awards, a few parts, many former crewmembers, photographs and a special place in American naval history. Only two memorials were left behind, one unofficial and one official: neither adequate, but both much better than nothing.

The unofficial memorial to *Enterprise* was the contribution of the overseer of the carrier's death. W. Henry Hoffmann was not only a friend to former Big E crewmembers, but also a friend to history. Hoffmann had the interest and foresight to cut out the rounded portion of the fantail upon which the *Enterprise* name was written on raised letters. Being approximately 16 feet long, over two feet high and weighing over a ton, the movement of the nameplate was no small project. Hoffmann offered the nameplate to the River Vale Township in New Jersey and the then mayor, Alfred C. Getler, not only accepted the offer but also took the time to organize an appropriate ceremony and make the dedicatory speech. The nameplate was installed by Mr. Hoffmann just behind a centerfield fence where his son, Carl, played Little League baseball. In time the park would be named for Mr. Hoffmann who died in 1965 while directing the demolition of elevated railways in Chicago. Today Mayor Getler is retired, but the nameplate remains. Thanks to Henry Hoffmann, Alfred Getler and River Vale, at least one significant part of the *Enterprise* hull remains.

Dedicatory plaque embedded in the base of Enterprise *Tower at the Navy-Marine Corps football stadium at the Naval Academy.*

Thomas Lake NAAA

Enterprise's *anchor on display at the Washington Navy Yard, Washington, D.C.*

PHAN Todd Beveridge, USN

Mr. Hoffmann also removed the three bulkheads upon which the carrier's war record had been painted and it was his intent to save them until history offered to take and place them in a proper memorial. However, history delayed in calling and after Mr. Hoffmann died the bulkheads were carried from his yard back to Kearny for disposal. By 1965 most all the paint had disappeared as the large bulkheads were necessarily stored outside and thereby exposed to the weather. One can see in the pictures presented herein that the bulkheads were in bad need of repainting even in 1958 when the pictures were taken. It may well have been that the paint was so far gone in 1965 that those who carried the famous war records away did not realize their value or even know what the bulkheads were. It is known that Mr. Hoffmann had personal plans for a memorial utilizing the bulkheads and other items if officialdom did not act.

In addition to his unofficial memorial of the nameplate, Mr. Hoffmann also contributed to the history of *Enterprise* with his photographs. Many of the photographs in these final two chapters were taken by Mr. Hoffmann, and they were taken for two reasons. One was to maintain a record for engineering purposes since the *Enterprise* demolition was a first and there would be need for lessons learned in the experience. Secondly, pictures were taken simply for remembrance; the several pictures appearing herein taken prior to the beginning of the destruction attest to his historical interest.

The pictures from the Hoffmann family collection were taken for the most part with an inexpensive family-type camera. Nonetheless, the quality was very good. Mr. Hoffmann was only an amateur photographer; his interest in taking the pictures was his subject, *Enterprise,* not photography. Although only a few of his pictures are present in this book, over 150 were taken and they record the entire dismantling process. In addition to the dismantling, his photographs show the condition of the ship in her last days—seaworthy, but visually in bad shape; an apparently ransacked hangar deck; relatively undisturbed flight-crew ready rooms; a painter's nightmare; and even in death, still majestic.

Location of two of the three war record paintings aboard Enterprise *in 1958.*   Hoffmann Collection

The only official memorial to *Enterprise* is the *Enterprise* Tower at the Navy-Marine Corps Stadium at Annapolis, Maryland which was discussed in the preceding chapter. The picture of the Tower in chapter 10 shows its location near the front gate of the stadium, and one can see at the bottom of the Tower the larger of the two plaques embedded therein. The other plaque is blocked from view by the shrubbery, but a close-up picture of one plaque is presented here. When the ceremonies were held to dedicate the Tower, several members of the *Enterprise* Association observed that the information on the war-record plaque was in error and changes were made.

Speaking of errors, the reader of this book has no doubt noted that the Congressional Record account of battle stars awarded to *Enterprise* was 18 of 22. In other places throughout this book the number awarded has been quoted as being 20. The correct number is 20, or 21 if the Class B award for sinking Japanese submarine I-70 is counted. The only ships near *Enterprise's* 20 (or 21) battle stars were cruiser *San Francisco* (CA-38) and destroyer *O'Bannon* (DD-450) with 16. The nearest carrier was *Essex* with 13. *Saratoga*, which began the war with *Enterprise* and served to the finish, received seven.

It must be mentioned that statistics available from U.S. Navy and other government sources often vary. Anyone who has spent time in Washington at the National Archives or Washington Navy Yard has run into this problem. The only consistent figures appear to be those estimating the number of ships and tonnages sunk by submarines. These primary source problems are understandable because the main business during wartime is not the keeping of statistics; confirmations of losses from the enemy are not available, and war does not lend itself to scorekeeping in the same manner one would score a baseball game. Quite often during the war it could not be determined exactly who should be credited for an enemy ship or plane, and many naval records were submitted by the ships, and whether intended or not, the "spirit of competition" is quite apparent in respective ship's accounts of their wartime exploits. Anyone researching statistics from ship's records in the World War Two era eventually raises the white flag of surrender when it becomes obvious that the entire Imperial Japanese Navy and Merchant Marine was sunk at least twice and all enemy planes were shot down three times more than the official count of 6,477.

The less-than-reassuring comments just mentioned to the contrary, we push on to look at the *Enterprise* record. The Big E did receive a wartime high 20 (or 21) battle stars. The only major battle stars she could have received but did not were (1) Battle of the Coral Sea when she was one day late, and (2) the Third Fleet Operations against Japan, 10

July-15 August 1945 when *Enterprise* was in Bremerton for kamikaze damage repair. *Enterprise* was the first aircraft carrier to receive the coveted Presidential Unit Citation and was the only carrier to receive both the Presidential Unit Citation and the Navy Unit Commendation during World War II. Other awards included: the Republic of the Philippines Presidential Unit Citation Badge, the Philippine Liberation Campaign Ribbon with one Bronze Star, the American Defense Service Medal and the World War Two Victory Medal. Also, in November 1945 when *Enterprise* was in Great Britain on one of her Magic Carpet voyages, the First Lord of the Admiralty made the first official Admiralty visit to an American warship and presented to the carrier an Admiralty pennant. Since the creation of the pennant during the 1588 defeat of the Spanish Armada, only one ship not a member of the Royal Navy has been honored by such a gift: *Enterprise.* Of all her awards and decorations, however, the one most appreciated by her crew was one she could not paint on a bulkhead: Secretary of the Navy Forrestal's 27 October 1945 statement that he would recommend to Congress that the ship be preserved as a national symbol, along with *Constitution* and *Constellation,* as "the one vessel that most nearly symbolizes the history of the Navy in this war."

Enterprise steamed over 275,000 miles in pursuit of the enemy during the war, registered 54,000 plane landings, was seriously damaged seven times and received structural damage on nine other occasions. The carrier claimed 911 enemy planes shot down by the ship's guns and planes, 71 ships sunk and another 192 damaged or probably sunk. Even if exact credit could be assigned to specific ships, *Enterprise's* total for enemy ships and planes probably would not have been the highest for carriers because *Enterprise's* 1944-1945 primary mission as a night operations carrier placed her essentially in a defensive role. Nonetheless, her totals were at or near the top, and the paramount consideration in the greatness of *Enterprise* was that she was THE carrier during the critical period of the war (1942), and her victories, whether against enemy carriers or planes, were then against Japan's best. Many "victories" for U.S. forces after October 1944 came against undefended or poorly-defended Japanese ships, and the quality of the bulk of Japanese pilots during and after the Marianas' "Turkey Shoot" was average to very poor. Many American pilots who fought the Japanese airmen throughout the war recall that the Japanese flight leaders were still good until near the end, but their wingmen were little challenge after late 1944. But, regardless of how the carrier may have ranked in plane and ship totals, her overall record speaks for itself. Indeed, for a Public Works Administration project she didn't do bad at all.

PROSPECTIVE MEMORIALS

The loss of *Enterprise* in 1958 set off a charge to save several other ships. State groups realized if a ship as notable as *Enterprise* could be lost, then there was little reason to believe other famous and not-so-famous ships would be preserved. Therefore, interested parties in several coastal states with port facilities to accommodate large ships came forward at the last moment to rescue a small group of World War Two vessels as state memorials. Battleships *Alabama*, *North Carolina* and *Massachusetts* joined the old *Texas* in escaping the cutters torch as patriotic citizens in these states mustered financial support from the private sector and enthusiastic moral support from their respective state governments. In later years interested parties in Charleston, South Carolina, began a successful effort to obtain as museums, old ships for the Patriot's Point Development Authority. To date Patriot's Point's most significant acquisition (in 1975) has been the second carrier *Yorktown* (CV-10) which received 11 battle stars in World War Two from 1943 through 1945 and four more for service off Vietnam.

Almost to a man, members of the *Enterprise* Association are pleased that ships like *Yorktown*, *Alabama*, *North Carolina*, *Massachusetts* and *Texas* have been preserved. Too, they appreciate the commemoration of the wreck of the battleship *Arizona* at Pearl Harbor, but in the interest of honesty they admit the loss of their ship and the subsequent preservation of ships that were not, as Secretary Forrestal said, "the one vessel that most nearly symbolizes the history of the Navy in this (WW Two)

Enterprise ship's bell at the U.S. Naval Academy. The bell is rung only after midshipmen victories over West Point.   Blackwood Collection

Enterprise (CV-6) nameplate in River Vale, New Jersey 1980.   Mayor Al Getler

The Avenger torpedo bomber debuted in June 1942 and thereafter served to the end of the war. The TBF designation meant the Avenger was produced by Grumman, the major producer. The TBM Avenger was produced by General Motors. King Collection

The F4U Corsair. Probably the most under-used fighter of the war. Available early in the war the Corsair was thought to have a landing speed too high for carrier decks. The gull-winged fighter, called "whistling death" by the Japanese, could fly farther and faster than any other WW Two Navy fighter and carried ordnance equal to or in excess of many bombers. King Collection

F4F Wildcat on display at the Naval Aviation Museum in Pensacola, Florida. The Wildcat fought through the entire war and was the only fighter to operate from Enterprise until late 1943. King Collection

The Douglas Dauntless SBD dive-bomber on display at the Naval Aviation Museum in Pensacola, Florida. The SBD, like the F4F Wildcat, fought through the war and flew from the Enterprise during the June 1944 Battle of the Philippine Sea. King Collection

The C. Wade McClusky Trophy on display at the Naval Aviation Museum, Pensacola, Florida. The trophy honoring the Enterprise pilot who made the momentous decision at Midway and led the attack on Akagi and Kaga is awarded each year to the outstanding attack squadron by the U.S. Navy. King Collection

Enterprise (CV-6) display at the Naval Aviation Museum, Pensacola, Florida 1981. King Collection

war," has left them with a deep hurt for many years. Not only have former *Enterprise* men been hurt but naval history lost a significant part of its past. The extensive conversions of the Essex-class carriers in the 1950s and the dismantling of most in recent years have left only eight carriers that served during World War Two, and all eight of these in no way resemble their World War Two appearance. With completely restructured islands, angle decks, enclosed bows, different elevator arrangements, removal of all WW Two guns and many other changes, the eight remaining carriers have essentially lost their World War Two historical interest. It must be noted, however, that the eight carriers just mentioned plus many other Essex-class carriers are or were famous in their own right, but still, only the preservation of *Enterprise* in 1958 would have maintained a World War Two aircraft carrier in the form of that era.

The fine naval historical center in Charleston, South Carolina may in time be the location of a memorial for *Enterprise*. Negotiations are still ongoing for a bronze plaque listing the several hundred *Enterprise* war dead to be placed aboard the *Yorktown*. Numerous other items from CV-6 may be added. Some of the items still extant from *Enterprise* in addition to the nameplate already mentioned are: the builders' plaque, a 15-foot high anchor, the ship's bell (presently at the Naval Academy and rung only when Navy beats Army in athletics), a wing from a Japanese plane shot down by the Big E, some deck planking, two flags flown during separate battles, anchor chain, a wardroom table, rudder angle, war plaques, trophies, two steering stands, funnel whistle and siren, clocks, some paintings and her logs (interesting reading in places—in addition to the many directional-change notations, there are unofficial entries such as eulogies to lost crewmembers, poems and several

quite un-Christian observations in regard to Tokyo Rose's seven different occasions of claiming *Enterprise* sunk). Several additional items are presently aboard the contemporary *Enterprise,* but the portholes, valve wheels and clocks on CVN-65 will probably remain there until that ship is decommissioned.

Although there are hopes a memorial aboard *Yorktown* in South Carolina and the *Intrepid* in New York City will materialize, the Enterprise Association is still seeking a location for a central memorial as opposed to the random displays of the carrier's memorabilia that do not adequately perpetuate memory of the ship. One of the prospective locations is the Enterprise Estate just outside Washingon, D.C. in Prince George's County, Maryland. This property originally belonged to *Enterprise's* first commander in 1938, Captain Newton H. White. Today, the Estate—house, grounds and adjacent golf course, is owned by the Maryland National Capital Park and Planning Commission. This beautiful property would be an ideal setting and negotiations are underway between the Association and the Prince George's County Department of Parks and Recreation. It was hoped that the nameplate in New Jersey could be moved to Enterprise Estate, but the Township of River Vale understandably has opted to keep the nameplate where it was placed by two of its own citizens. Still, there are tentative plans to round up as many as possible of the items mentioned earlier, perhaps add a replica of the Big E's distinctive 36-foot mast, commission a model builder to build a good-sized model of the carrier, perhaps someday acquire the nameplate from the present *Enterprise* (CVN-65), hold an appropriate ceremony, and have both the U.S. Navy and State of Maryland recognize Enterprise Estate as the official *Enterprise* Memorial.

Enterprise *(CVN-65), the world's first nuclear carrier.*   USNI

EPILOGUE

Why write a book on a 20,000-ton aircraft carrier that no longer exists? This question has been posed even by some who served, and a Marine Corps Colonel in 1962 once responded to this writer's question as to why the *Enterprise* was dismantled by stating that *Enterprise* was only steel and wood. But, there is another perspective.

Enterprise was a place. She was a place where men lived, fought and died. The Big E was the last piece of America many men were to see during their defense of the United States, and to many other men the dim, postage-stamp view of *Enterprise* on the horizon was the most beautiful thing they could hope to see after flying long hours to find the enemy, do battle with him, and then flying long hours again hoping to find the carrier, and to find her afloat and sufficiently undamaged to receive their plane aboard.

The United States is richer today because *Enterprise* did exist at a most appropriate time, and the country is poorer today because she was not preserved. As the one ship most symbolic of the U.S. Navy in World War Two, no other memorial can capture as much of the history of that era as that which was wrapped up in her. Most contemporary Americans cannot visit the battle sites of the Pacific war and cannot speak with those who defended their country at those sites. But *Enterprise* was there.

The record of the Big E's years in the Pacific read like a story-book saga of a lone fighter facing impossible odds. Born and tested in her season, she passed her test with distinction, and then like too many men who served aboard her, she died too soon.

Just as *Enterprise* deserves not to be forgotten, so too should her era not be forgotten. World War Two was the last war of its kind. Issues were clearly cut and the manner of battle depended upon the courage, sacrifice and commitment of individuals. In the present age issues often are not so clear cut and some believe pushbuttons have negated the role of individuals in war. However, the challenge of peace remains, and just as the United States and her former enemy Japan have been able to win the peace with each other, so now, as former Secretary of State Dean Rusk has often stated, "this generation must seek new answers to the perils that threaten the United States, and indeed, mankind."

Finally, present and prospective memorials to *Enterprise* have as their main purpose the remembrance of a proud time when an American generation made painful sacrifices that should not go unnoticed by benefiting generations. In today's world Americans must continue to vigilantly defend the legacy of peace and freedom for which such a high price was paid between 1941 and 1945.

"While conducting air operations south of Hawaii on 14 January 1969, a series of accidental explosions and fires damaged the after flight deck of the world's first nuclear carrier. The blast of nine bombs and resulting fires killed 27 and injured 65. Like Enterprise CV-6 *before her,* Enterprise CVN-65 *has known destruction and death."*

USN

-121-

APPENDIX

ENTERPRISE BATTLE STARS

USS ENTERPRISE and her Air Groups were awarded Campaign Stars on the Asiatic-Pacific Theatre ribbon for participation in the following engagements, operations and campaigns:

Pearl Harbor-Midway — 7 December 1941
  (Only planes which operated over Pearl Harbor)
Anti-submarine Action Class "B" Assessment
  — 10 December 1941
Pacific Raids — 1942
  Marshall-Gilbert Raids — 1 February 1942
  Air Action off Bougainville — 24 February 1942
  Marcus Island Raid — 4 March 1942
Battle of Midway — 3-6 June 1942
Guadalcanal-Tulagi Landings (Including First
  Salvo) 7-9 August 1942
Capture and Defense of Guadalcanal
  — 10-25 August 1942
Battle for Eastern Solomons (Stewart Islands)
  — 23-25 August 1942
Battle of Santa Cruz Islands — 26 October 1942
Battle of Guadalcanal (Third Savo)
  —12-15 November 1942
Rennel Island — 29-30 January 1943
Gilbert Islands Operation
  — 19 November - 4 December 1943
Marshall Islands Operation — 1944
  Occupation of Kwajalein and Majuro Atolls
  — 29 January - 8 February 1944
  Attack on Jaluit Atoll — 20 February 1944
Asiatic-Pacific Raids — 1944
  Truk Attack — 16-17 February 1944
  Palau, Yap, Ulithi, Woleai Raid
  — 30 March - 1 April 1944
  Truk, Satawan, Ponape Raid
  — 29 April - 1 March 1944
Hollandia (New Guinea) Operation
  —21-24 April 1944
Marianas Islands Operations — 1944
  Capture and Occupation of Saipan
  — 11-24 June 1944
  Battle of Philippine Sea — 19-20 June 1944
Western Caroline Islands Operation — 1944
  Raids on Volcano-Bonin Islands and Yap Island
  — 31 August - 8 September 1944
  Capture and occupation of the Southern Palau
  Islands — 6 September - 14 October 1944
  Assaults on the Philippine Islands
  — 9-24 September 1944

Leyte Operation — 1944
  Third Fleet Supporting Operations Okinawa
  Attack — 10 October 1944
  Luzon Attacks — 15, 17-19 October 1944
  Battle of Leyte Gulf — 24-26 October 1944
Luzon Operation — 1944-45
  Luzon Attacks — 6-7 January 1945
  Formosa Attacks — 3-4, 9, 15 January 1945
  China Coast Attacks — 12, 16 Janaury 1945
Night Carrier Group #90 Fifth Fleet Raids against
  Honshu and the Nansei Shoto in support of
  Iwo Jima Operation — 15-16, 25 February,
  1 March 1945
Assault and Occupation of Iwo Jima
  — 23 February - 12 March 1945
Okinawa Gunto Operation — 1945
  Fifth and Third Fleet Raids in Support of the
  Okinawa Gunto Operation — 17 March - 15
  May 1945

AIR GROUPS AND THEIR COMMANDERS ABOARD *ENTERPRISE* DURING WORLD WAR TWO

ENTERPRISE AIR GROUP
(7 December 1941 - 29 September 1942)
Commander Howard L. Young
Lt. Commander C. Wade McClusky
Lt. Commander Maxwell F. Leslie

AIR GROUP TEN
(10 October 1942 - 21 December 1943)
Commander Richard K. Gaines
Lt. Commander James A. Thomas

AIR GROUP SIX
(9 November 1943 - 16 July 1944)
Lt. Commander Edward H. "Butch" O'Hare
Lt. Commander John L. Phillips

AIR GROUP TEN
(24 December 1943 - 16 July 1944)
Commander Roscoe L. Newman
Commander William R. "Killer" Kane

AIR GROUP TWENTY
(4 August 1944 - 23 November 1944)
Commander Daniel F. "Dog" Smith

NIGHT AIR GROUP NINETY
(24 December 1944 - 16 May 1944)
Commander William I. Martin

ENTERPRISE CV-6
COMMANDING OFFICERS

Captain Newton H. White
— 12 May 1938 - 21 December 1938
Captain Charles A. Pownall
— 21 December 1938 - 21 March 1941
Captain George D. Murray
— 21 March 1941 - 30 June 1942
Captain Arthur C. Davis
— 30 June 1942 - 21 October 1942
Captain Osborne B. Hardison
— 21 October 1942 - 7 April 1943
Captain Carlos W. Wieber
— 7 April 1943 - 16 April 1943
Captain Samuel P. Ginder
— 16 April 1943 - 7 November 1943
Captain Mat B. Gardner
— 7 November 1943 - 10 July 1944
Commander Thomas J. Hamilton
— 10 July 1944 - 29 July 1944
Captain Cato D. Glover
— 29 July 1944 - 14 December 1944
Captain Grover B.H. Hall
— 14 December 1944 - 25 September 1945
Captain William A. Rees
— 25 September 1945 - 20 February 1946
Captain Francis E. Bardwell
— 20 February 1946 - 10 June 1946
Commander Conrad W. Craven
10 June 1946 - 31 January 1947
Commander Lewis F. Davis
— 31 January 1947 - 17 February 1947

SELECTED BIBLIOGRAPHY

BOOKS

Brown, David. *Aircraft Carriers.* New York: Arco Publishing Company, 1977.

Bryan, J. III. *Aircraft Carrier.* New York: Ballantine Books Inc., 1954.

Burns, Eugene. *Then There Was One.* New York: Harcourt, Brace and Company, 1944.

Bywater, Hector. *The Great Pacific War.* 1925.

Frank, Pat and Harrington, Joseph D. *Rendezvous at Midway: U.S.S. Yorktown and the Japanese Carrier Fleet.* New York: The John Day Company, 1967.

Friedman, Norman; Lott, Arnold S. and Sumrall, Robert F. *USS Yorktown (CV-10).* Annapolis: Leeward Publications, 1977.

Gordon, Gary. *The Rise and Fall of the Japanese Empire.* Derby: Monarch Books Inc., 1962.

Halsey, William F., and Bryan, J. III. *Admiral Halsey's Story.* New York: McGraw Hill, 1956.

Hara, Captain Tameichi. *Japanese Destroyer Captain.* New York: Ballantine Books Inc., 1961.

Inoguchi, Captain Rikihei, and Nakajima, Tadashi (with Roger Pineau). *The Divine Wind.* Annapolis: U.S. Naval Institute, 1958.

Ito, Masanori (with Roger Pineau). *The End of the Imperial Japanese Navy.* New York: W.W. Norton and Company, 1956.

Jackson, B.R., and Doll, T.E. *Douglas TBD-1 "Devastator."* Fallbrook: Aero Publishers, 1973.

Jones, Lloyd S. *U.S. Naval Fighters: 1922 to 1980.* Fallbrook: Aero Publishers, 1973.

Lord, Walter. *Day of Infamy.* Henry Holt Inc., 1957.

Lott, Arnold S., and Sumrall, Robert F. *Pearl Harbor Attack.* Annapolis: Leeward Publications, 1977.

Morison, Samuel Eliot. *The Rising Sun in the Pacific.* Vol. III: *History of U.S. Naval Operations in World War II.* Boston: Little, Brown and Co., 1948.

Morison, Samuel Eliot. *Coral Sea, Midway and Submarine Actions May 1942 - August 1942.* Vol. IV: *History of U.S. Naval Operations in World War II.* Boston: Little, Brown and Co., 1949.

Morison, Samuel Eliot. *The Struggle for Guadalcanal August 1942 - February 1943.* Vol. V: *History of U.S. Naval Operations in World War II.* Boston: Little, Brown and Co., 1949.

Morison, Samuel Eliot. *New Guinea and the Marianas March 1944 - August 1944.* Vol. VIII: *History of U.S. Naval Operations in World War II.* Boston: Little, Brown and Co., 1953.

Morison, Samuel Eliot. *Leyte June 1944 - January 1945.* Vol. XII: *History of U.S. Naval Operations in World War II.* Boston: Little, Brown and Co., 1958.

Morison, Samuel Eliot. *The Liberation of the Philippines 1944-1945.* Vol. XIII: *History of U.S. Naval Operations in World War II.* Boston: Little, Brown and Co., 1959.

Morison, Samuel Eliot. *Victory in the Pacific 1945.* Vol. XIV: *History of U.S. Naval Operations in World War II.* Boston: Little, Brown and Co., 1960.

Okumiya, Masatake, and Hirikoshi, Jiro (with Martin Caiden). *Zero.* New York: Ballantine Books Inc., 1957.

Pawlowski, Gareth L. *Flat-tops and Fledglings: A History of American Aircraft Carriers.* London: A.S. Barnes and Co., 1971.

Saki, Saburo and Saito, Fred (with Martin Caidin). *Samurai.* New York: Bantam Books, 1978.

Sowinski, Larry and Walkowiak, Tom. *United States Navy Camouflage of the World War Two Era.* Philadelphia: The Floating Drydock, 1977.

Stafford, Edward P. *The Big E.* New York: Random House, 1962.

Terzibaschitsch, Stefan. *Aircraft Carriers of the U.S. Navy.* New York: Mayflower Books, 1978.

Toland, John. *The Rising Sun.* New York: Random House, 1970.

Trumbull, Robert. *The Raft.* Camden: Henry Holt and Company Inc., 1942.

ARTICLES IN MAGAZINES

Dempewolff, Richard F. "The Big E Dies with Her Boots On." *Popular Mechanics,* May, 1960, pp. 65-70 and 236-238.

Morschauser, Joseph. "A Valiant Lady's Last Battle." *Look,* 5 March 1957, pp. 122-124.

Murphy, Frank L. "End of the Big E." *Bee-Hive,* Fall, 1958, pp. 8-12.

Rawlings, Charles A. "The Big E and the Divine Wind." *Saturday Evening Post,* 1 September 1945, pp. 9-11, 46-50.

"Turning Point in the Pacific." *All Hands,* July, 1962, pp. 59-63.

"U.S. Carrier is Bombed." *Life,* 14 December 1942, pp. 40-41.

PUBLIC DOCUMENTS

U.S. Congress, Senate. *Establishment of the U.S.S. "Enterprise" as a National Shrine in the District of Columbia.* S.J. Resolution 96, 1957.

UNPUBLISHED MATERIALS

Bulletins of the U.S.S. *Enterprise* Association

Deck Log of the U.S.S. *Enterprise* CV-6 (National Archives)